Anya -
thought you might
enjoy the read!

Universal Stretches

With Jay Paul

Written by Karen Barker

Copyright © 2006 by Karen Barker

ISBN 0-7414-3251-X

Janet McLeod, editor

Lee Simmons, cover design and photography

A kind thank you to the gang at UPS store, in Canmore for their patience.

Photo of Lyn Inglis and Karen Barker by Willy Fuder

Published by:

PUBLISHING.COM

1094 New DeHaven Street, Suite 100
West Conshohocken, PA 19428-2713
Info@buybooksontheweb.com
www.buybooksontheweb.com
Toll-free (877) BUY BOOK
Local Phone (610) 941-9999
Fax (610) 941-9959

Printed in the United States of America

Printed on Recycled Paper

Published July 2006

Contributions made by:
Lyn Inglis and Karen Barker.

Lyn is the medium that channels the
energy of Jay Paul, in harmony with
"Spiritual Stretches", from the higher aspect
of Karen Barker

A Dedication from Jay Paul

This book is dedicated to the great teachers that have manifested and brought light into the darkness with compassion and unconditional love and to all who are open to receive it.

Comments on the profound impact of
"Universal Stretches"

"Thank you so much for opening a door to a wonderful spirituality.

I express my gratitude to you both for teaching me how to trust in myself and allow the Universal energy or process to guide me on my journey."

Susan Buchik,
Special Needs Teacher

"Universal Stretches helps the lay person understand the dynamics of the ways of the universe. Jay Paul, Lyn and Karen offer an engaging discussion and insight about why world events have transpired and helpful hints about how we can adapt. I loved the 'spiritual stretches' – they help energize my soul"

Fiona Nicholson,
President of Contact Works/Life coach

"This text brings an understanding to all of Man kind. I anxiously await the next edition!"

Willy The Woodman,
Journeyman Carpenter

"Absolutely profound from the time I opened the cover to the very last page. Jay Paul has given us guidance to find our own true potentials on an individual basis and he has given us a worldly or global perspective of where the earth has come from and where it is going (especially by taking consideration of the tsunami and oil issues). We are entering into a New World and I look forward to the journey."

Susan

"I feel lifted up to a Higher View that simply and knowingly resonates as **Truth.** Reading this manuscript has enriched my understanding, given me tools to develop my intuition and somehow awakened a watchfulness for the beauty and grace in life. Thank you for stepping out in light and love, best of luck with the destination of this beautiful message."

Barbara Eastham, Yoga Instructor

Acknowledgments

A heart felt thank you to Lyn, Graham, Willy and Aly whose patience and support over this time was appreciated.

I would also extend this same gratitude to the Development Group of the fall of 2004, whose commitment to being all they can be in this lifetime has brought a deeper understanding to my purpose, for we have been each others teachers.

Blessings to my unseen friends of energy and light, who have come forward with their love and compassion, and have brought a deeper peace and healing in my life

A deep appreciation for Janet McLeod, as editor, whose patience in my learning curve was grace. Lee Simmons, as photographer and friend, your talent is an inspiration.

Blessings to those who journey into this book, may you find direction and insight knowing you are spiritual beings having a physical experience.

A Meditation

Lyn Inglis
Inspired by the Teachings
of Jay-Paul

Into Clear Light

Clear Light Meditation with Jay Paul

This was taped in a studio by Lyn Inglis. On the day, Lyn was quite nervous; it was her first experience at this. She went into that place of clear light and Jay Paul came through to do this recording in one take.

In studio terms, this means the first time was the right time. One did not have to redo anything. The music and graphics were chosen next by Lyn.

What a beautiful experience to be able to create so purely in that space. A wonderful reflection on how living life in this third dimension can be.

In doing this meditation I would suggest that you find a quiet place and allow at least 45 minutes the first time you do it. Once you learn how to journey into the frequency of clear light or of your original nature it will accessible to you anywhere and any time.

The journey I have had in doing this has been evolving as I have grown and opened. I invoke the energies of my higher self and Jay Paul. Some times I put an intention out for healing or clarity pending on what is happening in my life or what I may be processing. If I seek peace I state that before entering into the meditation.

I allow myself to let go with all the fibers of my being to enter into the experience before me. Each time it is unique for me. As each moment I am ever evolving, for example, cells are always dying and regenerating on a physical level.

With the development groups, Lyn Inglis and I ask that the group members do the CD three times a week for three weeks before we meet so everyone has a shared common ground.

Jay Paul refers to the CD meditation on Page 15 of this book.

Please access www.lyninglis.com or www.jay-paul.com for purchase of this CD.

Blessings to you,

May the light of the universe always be with you.

Part One

Healing Within Individual Issues

Chapter One

Understanding Energies

I feel honored and full of joy at the opportunity I have been given to share my journey and understanding with you regarding Jay Paul's messages to humanity.

Lyn Inglis is the medium whom Jay Paul, as she calls him, channels through. One must know that there are many mediums as in John Edwards, James Van Praagh who re unite loved ones that have passed over for healing as well as for direction and guidance in ones life. Lyn does the same sort of work. For more information go to www.lyninglis.com

Lyn has a wonderful gift that she was blessed with from birth. As she channels Jay Paul her energy actually leaves her physical body and the spirit known as Jay Paul comes into her physical being. Lyn's eyes are usually closed and when Jay Paul is present the energy does move her arms, drinks water, smiles, laughs, nods her head, everything but stands up and walk around. It is a unique experience to be able to be present through this process. Lyn often says she goes somewhere that is so beautiful, warm and peaceful she has a hard time wanting to come back.

As she re enters her physical body she needs several minutes to adjust to the weightiness she feels in physical form. I am not sure whether you have done meditation, but when you have finished a deep meditation as in a deep sleep very often as you get up to walk your legs feel heavy or you feel disoriented. That is the same in her experience.

So with that understanding, though it maybe new to you, I bless you for opening your hearts to journey through this book that encompasses many levels of understanding from the universal perspective, Jay Paul's perspective as spirit.

His simple and profound message is that if we can open our hearts as humanity to listen to the Earth and each other not through our ears but with our whole being then we can open our minds to the vastness and expansiveness of who we are. For in universal understanding we are the sum of all of our experiences. All our experiences through many lifetimes are not wasted and the knowledge of the universe is within us all. I know you are teaming with questions and hopefully the light of the universe will shine within you and the understanding will unfold as you journey through this text.

My advice if you are at the level of understanding where you can allow yourself to be in that quiet place within as you journey and experience these words that would be wonderful. If you consider yourself a beginner or novice and are curious just allow yourself to relax and with an open mind only accept what is acceptable to you and let the rest go.

As an introduction to the time and place around the following taped discussion, Lyn and I have been running two Intuitive Development Groups. In these groups we focus on healing our resistant energies so that more of the light if you can call it that or lightness starts to fill our lives. The anger, pain, and frustration that life deals us on a daily basis can be managed or ultimately transformed so we can keep centered. These emotions that we experience, that throw us off our center, we will call lower vibrational or the denser energies. There has been scientific proof through specific testing of our DNA that love is the highest vibration as opposed to fear. Gregg Braden has done most of this research. You can access more information at www.greggbraden.com.

Look at the colors of the rainbow. Beautiful as they are, each color of the rainbow vibrates to a different frequency. As do the emotions, red being the lowest and violet being the highest vibration the same as fear versus love. In healing the resistant energies which can act as obstacles in our lives, we then create more space for the love and light allowing the sense of freedom which as spiritual beings having a physical experience is an environment we need so we can flourish. There is truth to cleaning up the negative thought patterns in our life so that we can learn or remember to celebrate life with the joy filled celebration of being here.

Many books have been written exploring this topic. One that comes to mind is "The Power of Positive Thinking". Also, each person has a unique ability regarding developing their intuition. Very often we see images, colors, hear messages or we can sense heat, cold, energy changes in a room. In the groups we spend time exploring each ones gift and giving specific exercises to develop it.

The groups of people that are participating in this discussion have also focused their energies on global healings. Some of the participants are in the healing profession, an acupuncturist, psychiatrist, massage therapist, a few are moms, and there is a couple who are expecting their first born child, a carpenter and an accountant. A good percentage of this group is self employed as well.

We meet once a week for two hours over a structured time frame, which maybe 12 weeks or 6 weeks pending on the time of year. This specific group has been together over the full year. Two members that work in the healing arts have come into this 12 week run as new members. They have a knowing of energy so it worked that they be present.

I bless and honor them for journeying with me and contributing to my personal growth.

My additions to the script will be in Italics.

Spiritual Stretches

We are going to do a little warm up for those beginners joining us in this experience.

My hope is that in sharing these stretches one can go within to get re-connected with all of who we are and come to the realization that we are all interconnected and inter dependent in that spiritual understanding. Many times in this third dimension we reach for what is tangible because of our experience here on Earth. I, with love and compassion, share these spiritual stretches that reach inward to explore who we are within. For within ourselves is where the healing begins as we awaken to our fullest potential that we are all spiritual beings having a physical experience

These are a few stretches that have affected my life profoundly with their simplicity. Done as frequently during the day they have transformed my life or reality in to a heaven on Earth. The illusion of living in pain and sickness has not served one of us and to experience home here on Earth is a deep peace that only the soul can know. Its expansive knowledge will embrace all who ask for it. It is like a veil that needs to be lifted and all is one. The healing of duality and separation is integral within us and of this world to evolve to what we all are. The cosmos and spiritual energies all aid in transmuting and transforming the density so we may rejoice in light to a life of peace and grace for all. The struggle will end and the love that surrounds us and has surrounded us always will now be felt and experienced. In peace and unity please join me in these simple ways of transforming or re-claiming the journey as divine beings that we all are.

Feeling Energy

As we begin, it is important to know we all can feel the energies around us. The wonderful feeling when you encounter something in Mother Nature that speaks to you like a beautiful tall tree you feel drawn to eat your lunch under on a sunlit day or the joy the gentle rain gives you as it dances off your skin or window pane wherever you may be. Being in a room with those you love, feeling the safety and peace it brings you as opposed to entering a room with a group of people you may not know and sensing who you feel drawn or safe to sit beside, as you wait in a doctor's office, are all examples of how we use energy.

We all know what it feels like when we avoid sitting beside a person or energy that gives us the No feeling. In simple terms you have just had an awareness of energies around you. All these observations or responses are responses to energy that we or others hold.

A simple exercise to help you get a tangible experience of energy is, place your hands about 6 inches apart then bring them slowly together then apart. You may feel a tingling or some resistance as you bring them together and apart several times. That is your energy. We all have energy fields that surround us as well. When we feel heat from someone's hands as they touch us or hold a part of our physical body that is in pain is a form of healing energy coming from them. It always feels peaceful and comforting never invasive.

When my daughter was younger, I described it as having the "Yes feeling" or "No feeling" from someone. This gave her a simple vocabulary to share her thoughts or perceptions of people.

Start from this moment forward to incorporate this awareness in your daily life. Notice those that give you the Yes or No feeling, knowing that your personal radar is communicating to you, and then the next part of the learning curve is to trust it. That is where healing the resistant energies will serve the purpose as part of the steps of the journey in awakening the healing within.

As we plant that seed and watch it grow we learn more about the plant. Be patient, for sometimes when the plant grows it is imperceptible to us. Trust in the process, for the plant's stem will come, then the leaves, and in time, the flower.

Chapter Two

With love I give you Jay Paul.

My Friends, Thank you for allowing me to come into this session with you. I am known as Jay Paul and I know there are some of you I have met and some of you are new to meeting of my energy, as such. What I want to explain to you, if I may do so, is that I am known to Lyn as Jay Paul. I come to her as many energies combined together to try and bring some understanding into the process of spirit to those who are open to receiving this information.

If I were to try to describe myself it would be complicated to do that in the physical sense, for I am made up of many millions of different types of energy far beyond that which you would fully understand. I work only for the highest universal good and purpose. But I come through as one person, as Lyn can identify with that. My work is not just limited to working with one individual but I work with several hundred in this way around the world and in different ways and they all know me as different things. And yet I am all that is complete as you are and I am everything that is and always has been.

I work primarily through Lyn, with her, in helping other people realize their spiritual, emotional and physical potential. My journey is different than yours for I have chosen to do this to work from this spiritual existence to send energy through spiral systems down towards the Earth as the Earth goes through its own period of changes. For we are all interdependent on each other, every sentient being, every sentient life form is part of this energy that we share. Lyn came into your world with the predetermined gift of working with energy to be able to support our work, as many others have chosen this too.

The Earth has given itself to mankind, and to sentient beings, to provide an environment where one can be limited in a physical existence, a third dimensional existence, and learn to be able to deal and cope with the different environments, different changes and different situations in ones life. You cannot learn to do things in a physical manner in a higher dimensional frequency because the energy or vibrations are too light or you may say too high to hold the denser energies.

What is it like being in spirit as opposed to on Earth in physical form? Do you feel pain, or make love?

On the Earth plane you can learn to start with a clean slate, and learn through what you truly are by experiencing the process of change by connecting more fully in nature. Here in spirit, in this dimension, you can be many things at the same time for we are multi dimensional and limited by linear laws. On Earth, you can be physical, you can touch and feel, you can experience physical emotions; you can be spiritual and compassionate with in your physical body. You can know pain in a different way to how you know it in spirit. For on Earth things evolve in a linear fashion. It is though being here on Earth, that you have to learn to deal with time which only exists in this frequency and dimension, this that allows you to experience the process of being born and going through life in different experiences that create the opportunity for you to grow in a unique way. Also you experience what it is like to leave the Earth frequency, as you are transported back to your original spiritual nature. When you are in a higher frequency, the experience is different. You do not have to leave the physical body. But within a physical body you can learn what it is to love on that level of being and to integrate that on a spiritual and emotional understanding.

In the physical world you use your senses to see, hear, smell, taste, and touch. Here you can see things in motion actually happening. Where as in a higher frequency we are in a position where thought is reality and reality is instantaneous, so you do not have to go through the motion of putting things together. Third dimensional energy is limiting but it provides an incredible environment for you to learn, to suffer, to love, to have loss, and to find joy again.

The cycle of life in the third dimension propels itself in a way for you to experience many different things to help you evolve. Remember too that the Earth is its own life force and it too evolves. It has offered itself to us over millions of years to experience physical life. Over many thousands of years man has abused this wonderful resource and now it has manifested in the need for change. As you are aware in your world, when you see the script that has been written, the text that has been printed, and if you look at your electric and electronic technology, you will see there are things that are happening now on the Earth are a build up of negative energy that pertains to thousands of years. It is now time for that energy to start to change. I am not saying that this is not something that has not happened before for there are many Earth energy shifts in your history. Every day seismic events show this. But never before have the changes been so rapid, this will unfold more obviously over the next few years. I am not talking of Armageddon for that is based in ignorance and on fear. I am talking about the understanding of healing; unconditional love and compassion to become the main focus, so you can once and for all stop the energies propelling that make a living hell on Earth for those that suffer. Turn that energy into a positive frequency and make heaven on Earth for all sentient beings, the Earth included.

Heaven on Earth? Who will teach us?

We no longer send one ambassador from spirit or one teacher as you have seen in the past. For that which came before was turned into a different understanding by mankind

11

so that particular individuals could change the truth into a means of control. That was never the intention of the great master teachers or the universe. The truth that was altered by man kind deflected from the teachings of universal law of love, compassion and forgiveness and turned it into a means to control for personal gain. Now many are coming into your world with an innate understanding that we need to remember our original nature, our true selves, and our universal aspect and bring that into being. For that is unconditional love and compassion at work. If we all listen to that aspect of ourselves we can change things that are happening now in this world. Bring in the understanding of remembrance that you are spiritual beings having a physical experience. And that you have chosen to be here in this time frame limited that it is, so that you can help the Earth itself on its journey through change.

Why should we spend the time exercising our intuition?

Through heightening of your own intuition to connecting with that universal energy that you are all a part of, you can raise the collective consciousness of yourselves and those around you. To understand that there is greater purpose in all things than you usually see on a daily basis. The Earth is going through this cycle of change, it has begun and it is propelling itself over the next few years. You may have noticed around you many changes in the way that you as a species react and exist. You will notice that people at this time are fragile as though there is awareness that things need to be completed. The result of cause and effect allows different energies to pertain to different individuals. That is why in the denser energies on Earth, people are making the choice to literally die for their beliefs. This causes confusion and results in an imbalance of energy around those affected. It is as though they are racing to the finishing line and not understanding, life as they experience it. The remembrance of who they really is forgotten. No questions are asked, the negative energy just drives individuals down a one way street. No one looks back and asks "what if" or says "I can stop this madness". Where these denser energies are playing out there is destruction and war, famine and disease. And that is causing psychological, emotional and physical problems both in individuals and the Earth itself. It is also a sign of spiritual disconnection to the universe truths.

So with raising your own intuition and connecting more fully with what you truly are, then you use your energy to help people and those around have a greater understanding what is before them. If you reach out to try to heal the blocks that stop yourselves and others from moving forward into the higher frequencies of unconditional love and compassion then you are helping to bring about a wonderful change, for the law of cause and effect works on all levels, whether negative or positive. So I honor you all for being here, being part of this group for you have chosen this human experience as well as many other lifetimes to bring you to this place of having the opportunity for propelling and living with a positive change. You have chosen to bring light into the darkness.

The job is hard! I find myself disconcerted in these times.

I would share with you my understanding that not all universal energies choose a human form, or a sentient form of existence, as you understand it, as it is known to be a hard journey. For it is not something we do only once, it is likening to you signing a contract to go through millions of life times and energies of experiences that bring knowledge to add to the universal growth of the experiences of all life itself.

Look upon yourselves as being your own universe. Look upon your spacious compassionate heart as being the centre of that universe. Let every atom in your body outside of that spacious heart have its own energy field all interdependent on each other and yet still sustainable. Every form of life is like this. Look at the night sky and you will get an understanding of what I am trying to portray here. You have chosen to manifest your own universe if you will. Through your compassionate heart and your universal experiences you grow in purpose. You learn awareness, to wake up and gradually reach into enlightenment, then you can share that knowledge with all life. It is through this process the universal mind grows. Like us the universe is the sum of all our experiences.

It is known to be a tough journey, a hard journey and so we honor those that chose it. For it brings anguish, it brings pain, it brings suffering, and it brings loss. Through all those things you find out truly what you are outside of the human form, outside of your existence. We can only grow and learn about love and compassion through our suffering and pain. We can only find compassion through our own experiences, and then we should be able to share it freely with the world.

We cannot do that in the same way in spirit. It is something that pertains and manifests only in third dimensional energy. There are other worlds and other places that I can talk to you about but I don't think that's relevant for now.

With all that is happening many of us can feel so alone in this world.

But you are not alone in your existence and I wish to share that understanding with you, for you are part of I, and I am part of you and we are all as one. We all are interdependent upon the universe and our own growth.

So within yourselves within your own healing journeys remember that you are your own universe. Your heart is the center of that universe. Extending from that, every atom within you is like a star in the night's sky. Each atom is brilliant. It carries the life force of creation itself within it. It carries the DNA of the universal beings, as well as to your physical being. When the time comes for you to leave your Earthly existence, and for your energy to change, it is as though you just unravel yourself and that inner nature that heart of compassionate energy is what continues. That is what is eternal; that is what is infinite. It is not something just of the human nature. Your compassionate heart, as I would like to think of it, your inner soul, or spirit, is that which has manifested itself through all things and all experiences. It is not the physical heart, it is your universal being, that part of you that is infinite.

Clear Light Meditation

I would like to bring some bearing of understanding of some of the exercises that you have shared and I have been aware of. With practice you have been aware that you have been able to change your frequency on some level within yourself, and place yourselves in that frequency that we call "clears light". You will understand in this mediation that you feel totally free. You are liberated, when you go to this place inside of yourself which is beyond human form. Even though you are still encased by the human body, you are aware of emotionally and spiritually being in a different frequency. In itself this is like experiencing a "mini death" as you would call it in the physical sense, because you have actually transcended physical energy when you have that experience. So with explaining that to you I hope that can take away any fear you might have of change of energy within your own lives (dying), for it is as normal as the breath you breathe every day to keep you alive in the physical form. To manifest energy to open up into a higher frequency should be as easy as that. When you are in touch with your intuition, when you are in touch with your compassionate heart, when you are in touch with your

15

universal being, when you are in touch with your original nature, you can transcend all things.

You may wonder what part this plays in your life or what you have to offer. But I am not throwing it out there that you are going to change the world in one breath or one word (although from that place of clear light, you do have the ability to do so). As a group of beings working together or even as individuals if you use this knowledge to share with even one person you will bring some light into their darkness. If you can help them find within themselves that place of knowing and truth, they can let go of their fears. They can then reach out to explore their potential and in doing so find joy, peace, truth, and understanding of their place within the universe. They can become authentic in their understanding of love as it is truly meant to be.

For that is the reason for our being. If you can walk the talk and project your energies to this purpose into light then that is all you have ever been asked to do and to be done. So that if you recognize that within yourselves you can make a difference in helping yourselves and all life you can see you really can make a difference. This understanding is your universal birthright; don't be afraid to use it.

I do not want to sit and just talk on this level for I know that there are those here who share that understanding I just wish to bring some confirmation with it. I have been aware of your energies in the last few weeks as you have come together as a group and grown and I am excited for you for what you are feeling at that level of your being physically, emotionally and spiritually.

I hope I haven't dumbfounded you all.

(There is general laughter as Jay Paul's humor is evident. In spirit, I have discovered humor is very necessary.)

Healing Resistant Energy or Recycling Emotions

The resistant energies that we hold in our body or mind is like a contraction. It can create illness; make us feel unwell mentally or in our thoughts. Clearing ourselves, acknowledging them in our patterns is the first step to be able to open fully to our hearts to listen. The denser energies, as in fear, will attract the same vibration, fear. It is time to awaken to different choices that will serve our highest purpose. Imagine what it would like to experience the joy everyday of being alive. For some of us it is a dream. For some of us we have worked hard to be there. I am joy. On the Earth as we know it now, there are the denser energies that are playing out in magnitude. So I have great compassion with myself as a spiritual being in this physical experience for that. It seems hard to feel free. The resistance is global and in humanity a thousand fold but in this book it is an awakening to choose differently. As we do our daily exercises we can also incorporate our daily spiritual stretches to fully enhance ourselves. Be patient and compassionate with yourselves on your new journey as you grow.

The Dalai Lama makes reference to the fact that there is no word in the English language for self-compassion. If the journey starts within, the compassion needs to start from within.

I bless you on this journey. I ask the universe for its love, protection and direction at all times.

Start allowing yourselves to bless everything that comes into your path or enters your consciousness. For example, bless the highway as it gets you to work, bless the bird that thought of poverty or struggle, bless that thought of joy, bless the coffee, bless the chocolate, bless the Soya milk. Allow yourself to be creative and witness how you see things start to change.

Jay Paul, advised me to clear the self-judgment and fear that was within me creating obstacles in my ability to fully come into what, I can see from this place in time, is the next stage of my journey. He was very emphatic and I knew he was offering me some essential guidance but in retrospect I wasn't sure how I was going to do it. He shared that in spirit no energy judges another for their choices for it is all experience. Judgment has been created in my humanity in the third dimensional frequency. The old dynamic that I was running negative thought processes was causing huge contractions inside me thus preventing the light and my personal growth.

I turned to Lyn who taught me, in the moment acknowledge the emotion, feel it for it is mine then send the energy up to my minds eye where I can express my disappointment or frustration in having to work through this yet again. After having owned the self-judgment in its entirety I brought the energy into my heart surrounding it with love and compassion transforming the vibration which is what it felt like into a lighter vibration love or compassion then exhale the whole experience. I would go inside again and see as to whether it had truly gone or I had to do the process again.

Very often in the beginning I had to recycle this emotion once, twice or three times depending on my state. I had to cultivate self compassion in a disciplined way. Now after a few years of doing this I can honestly say it comes as an involuntary response when I experience any feelings that are lower in vibration.

So I ask you to do some searching as to what your resistant energies are and be diligent in transforming them because the reward is freedom. As Thich Nhat Hanh says, we are more than our feelings.

Sit in meditation stance or in a quiet place and find the stillness. If you have a hard time letting an emotion go, for example, I feel...disappointment. Bring the emotion up to the mind's eye and say, "I am so tired of dealing with this, I am angry at his choice to send that controlling energy at me." As a spiritual being having this physical experience I have huge love and compassion for myself at having to experience this. I surround the energy with love as I say these words and I connect with my higher self. I then embrace my physical self, and exhale. I re-evaluate. If I feel at peace, I give thanks and bless the moment of peace. As I breathe in, I feel peace, as I breathe out, I smile at my body's peace.

Resistant energies attract resistant energies. This is why it is so important we release these so the light and higher vibrational feelings such as love and kindness can be with us more frequently. Those higher vibrations attract higher vibrations and that is when we can start to see our world shift. The people we meet will start to change as we attract those that are more in tune with our interests. We may feel our job or wardrobe shifting because we desire from our hearts differently. I went from wearing black, navy, to colors that were brighter white, gold and blues. These hold the resonance of emotional healing. Allow this and bless the process knowing the work you are doing is serving you. For energy is never wasted.

Virus and bacteria have been born and breed in the lower frequencies. In your meditation ask "to raise my frequency to the precise vibration so that virus or bacteria cannot live in my physical body". Virus and bacteria can only survive in the lower frequencies or the denser vibrations. It has its own purpose. We need to raise our level of understanding so that the virus and bacteria can not exist within us. As Sam Graci writes in "Super foods" there is scientific evidence that thought, yoga, meditation can change the alkalinity in our bodies so we can be healthier. Acidity in our bodies causes joints to be arthritic and various other pathologies. Acidity can be nurtured by negative thoughts, foods; choices we make that do not serve our highest good. One can go into a health food store and purchase the test paper that Greens Plus makes which is a tool to test the urine in the a.m. for its acidity. It's great and tangible.

Keep pure thoughts by listening to music or singing mantras.

For example, the Dalai Lama always starts his day with, Ohm mane pad me ohm. Robert Thurman's book "Circling the Sacred Mountain" has a fabulous dissertation on the meaning of that mantra.

Chapter Three

An invitation to ask questions

Jay-Paul: I wish to know if there is anything that I can add or contribute to your coming together. If there are any questions I can answer for you I would be happy to do this. Anything you may wish to ask. Is there anybody that can speak forward?

Karen: There are a few people that had questions prepared for you a few weeks ago, Jay Paul.

Jay Paul: Would they be able to speak up? Mary, if I may approach you on this Mary as there doesn't seem to be anybody else that is ready to speak at present. I want you to know that I am approachable for I speak as one individual to you as another, that we share the same energy. There is no difference from each other, we are just working in a different place.

(He is truly letting everyone know and inviting them that we are all equals. This is the first time this group has met with Jay Paul and has been part of this experience. We have also worked at connecting with our guides or guardian angels, if you would call it that. For some the journey has been an easy one, others have had a difficult time connecting either out of self doubt or lack of clarity. This is a perfect opportunity to ask and know within you what is true. Sometimes the information doesn't come because it is not the right time and we need to honor that.)

Mary, in regard to your connection with your guide, regard to your whole spiritual experience of evolving maybe I can address this with you. The path that you have chosen was originally traditional with sense of your community and the culture in which you were raised. You have chosen in your later life, as your experiences have grown, and as you have seen the suffering of others, to reach inside yourself to find different answers, to try to make sense of the chaos you see from day to day in your work.

You have brought into your understanding a universal expression of being. You are able to connect with a greater understanding that life is a commitment to experience. You have offered yourself selflessly in a way that can help others move forward, by helping them remove their own blocks and the things that are holding them back.

I have watched you and seen you grow in great beauty in understanding the universals process. Even though you may struggle from time to time with your own interpretation of the energies I want to honor you for what you have done and the role you play in other people's lives. You connect very fully with the healing energies that are around you. You have, if you like, the thread of the universe you need to help you with your work. You have the understanding of the fabric of the universe, as I call it. You take what you need from your experiences, in this life time, and from other experiences, where you can use that thread as a tool to help other people to be able to fix what is wrong with them, being able to help them look inside themselves to see the reality of their being.

You are surrounded by many who are there to help you on this journey. I spoke to Lyn earlier on and I believe as she mentioned to you I bring to you the Buddha of understanding The Medical Buddha, the Medicine Buddha as you know it. I bring it to you in the energy of sapphire blue because of the nature of the work that you chose to do. Blue is a healing color, it is a healing color of the emotions; it is a healing of the spirit not just the physical. You are able to take the information from your universal understanding as well as that which you have learned practically and you are able to reach out and help others come to terms with your interpretation of their energy.

That is the blue light that surrounds you and that is why I bring you the blue sapphire Buddha as that to be your mentor and your teacher. I hope that is acceptable to you. It also goes with your energy, your own field of being. Your own personal aura energy is basically blue and green. Which are the healing colors? I also have watched to as you have worked through these last few days with Steven and his interpretation of the energy fields. I just ask you to continue to reach out in that greater understanding it will bring you more evidence to what is real. What is reality and what isn't? So trust your intuition you don't have to second guess it. Let that energy flow through you as best that it can. Thank you for being here. Thank you for connecting.

Chapter Four

Jay Paul: Is there any other that would ask me a question?

(Janet, a mother of an autistic child, asks a question regarding what she can do to help her autistic son who is 6 years old.)

I understand the interpretation of what you ask. I can only tell you that through the experience of being the mother of your child here, through the experience of choice before you came into this life time, you chose the role that you are perusing now. You are his mother for purpose.

The New Children

I have talked before to you on some level about the need of this energy that is coming into the world known as Indigo Children. These children carry the light of the future ways rather than past experiences. The collective conscious is higher. I know there are many different interpretations of indigo children. In the right homes where they are honored and helped they fly free and strong. In homes that limit them they can become difficult and are often misdiagnosed.

Your son comes into this lifetime with that understanding but he is also limited in resource with that mental capacity to absorb all that is around him. The best way you can reach out and help him within your own understanding is to follow your intuition into your being and into his and to read his energy as it is, rather than to change it.

You need to encourage him to be able to concentrate on what it is that drives him initially. You need to help him look within himself for why he is here. You need to give him direction when he is able to take it. In understanding that he is part of some thing far greater and he need not be limited by his condition. For in some aspects this adds something to his being for he chose this limited understanding as well. For you to be able to reach out and encourage him to become all that he can be will help him incredibly.

Help him get in touch with the nature of energy that exists around him. Don't limit him or try to change him too greatly. Connect him very much with the energy of the Earth for that is healing. Teach him about the world and what grows there. Teach him to be able to plant a seed and watch it grow, to nourish it, and to help it. He may not be able to find the right words but show him that sometimes it is o.k., that certain things are beyond his expression, but he can still identify them within his own heart. You can give him that stimuli, you need to show him ways he can exhibit his own gifts and use them.

As I say touch base with the Earth energy around him so that will help. Also with understandings that as I can give to you his condition will change as he matures. Once he is able to concentrate more fully you will better understand the nature of whom and what he is. There are other ways that you can work with him and get specialized help if you need to in the next few years. But again I say do not take away from him that which is truly his. That is the foundation of why he is on this journey that is his choice to be this way. Encourage him in all the things that bring him peace. Encourage him in music and movement. Also show him a way to direct his inward intensity, work with energy like you have within this group with vibration and see if that starts to change something within him. Janet, it will be something that he can identify with.

You will see as I say as he progresses further into adulthood that some of the things that hold him back will be lessened. He will be more outgoing in a way of acceptance of others around him. There is some confusion within him at the moment with energies that used to be around him and now have left. He manifests things too through other people's energies, when he picks up on, but does not always understanding. He is very sensitive so teach him to be able to protect his energy field. Teach him not to take on that which is not his and not to be influenced by it. Teach him to be strong. But overall teach him that his choice in this lifetime for what he is and what will become is okay. Honor him for that. That is the best way you can help him.

I don't know if this makes sense to you or not but I ask you to try those things. I also ask you not to give him a projected thought of your own processes for what you feel he is. Rather encompass him with great compassion and love and understanding for who he truly is.

Janet: Thank you

I have been blessed with raising an Indigo Child. The term came from a color that was showing up as pre dominant in their auras or energy fields thus the term Indigo, related to the third eye or sixth charka of foresight. As Jay Paul has mentioned the energy is connected with a direct knowing who they are and their purpose, the fifth dimensional frequency or our higher selves. I have explored many ways to support my daughter's journey in reading implementing activities and discussing quite openly universal concepts which she responds to very easily. These energies need the freedom of expression to be present in the physical body so let's start with singing.

Sing your thoughts whenever the opportunity presents itself. For the voice and frequency begins inside. The cathedral of our mouths is directly related to the brain. Let that frequency travel and reverberate through out the brain and body out into your environment. I love when my daughter chooses to sing in her baths. It is a wonderful reflection of her personal freedom of expression. The soul and spirit are united in song. Dr. Doreen Virtue author and psychologist who has created the term "Angel Therapy" says, where there are people singing, there are the angels. Her book entitled "Angel Medicine" journeys into the minerals of the Earth and her remembrances of healing in the time of Atlantis, where sound and frequency were primarily used for healings in the temples. The message from the Stonehenge Stones is that is very important that humanity reclaims their powers to heal themselves and to manifest.

Ask that ease and grace surrounds you and the joy filled celebration of being here graces you daily.

One may use Celtic sea salt or table salt which is also known as white light. It is a crystal and the denser energies can not be anchored when that is present. Sprinkle it around the perimeter of your home, at the windows or over your bed. I found with my daughter teaching her these simple ways empowered her. Then she felt more at peace, if she suffered from nightmares or didn't feel comfortable. Using candle light, flowers, minerals such as crystals and incense, they will anchor in the higher vibrations. Incense has a two fold purpose, as an offering and also in Chinese Medicine the herbs are inhaled through the lungs which can be beneficial for healing. That is why to use natural ingredients is so important or essential oils that are pure. These affect us physically as well.

These simple skills shared with our children are priceless. My daughter comes home after school and usually has a bath with incense or candlelight on her own initiative to help with clearing her of all the energies she has encountered in her day as well as to center herself.

Surround your home with the violet flame running constantly. This is a good clearing and protection technique as well. Take time and implement it around your child's school, office or local hospital.

Try playing music that calms or clears like the sound of the Tibetan bowl or Ohm chanting is great to quickly shift the energies in your office or home. It clears the resistant energy.

Tibetan bowls, Tinshaws or other instruments that create a high frequency are fabulous for clearing and centering of the energies that surround you. The sound will present itself differently in tone if there is denser energy in that area. So with working in clearing and re balancing, listen with your human and etheric ear. Allow yourself to experience in your body the frequencies and sound. It will break up the lower frequencies not harmonious with you and then release them from your physical body.

When using my bowl to clear some energy on a client one day the energy came out of the bowl and physically grazed the side of my face. I felt it like a force missing the side of my face as in a hit, a comet of energy.

Plants are wonderful. Some absorb negative energies as in the spider plant. I had one spider plant near my bed where one leaf would vibrate. The spider plant has hundreds of long leaves, so for one to vibrate it is for purpose. As soon as I would acknowledge it and connect with its meaning it would instantly stop. It usually had a message for me with regards to increasing protective energy.

Doreen Virtue's book "The Care and Feeding of Indigo Children" is a fabulous "to do" book.

Chapter Five

(Lee is the expecting father who is self employed as a photographer. His homeland is Australia. He asks a question regarding information on inspiration and manifestation. He has just set up two offices in small towns that are close by.)

Jay Paul: I am going to approach this to you from a slightly different way from how you have explained it to me. Perhaps we can meet somewhere in the middle. Let's first of all talk about inspiration, the two different types of inspiration that you work with in the human form. You have talked within our group of the understanding of these two different forms of inspiration. Inspiration "means from a higher source". Inspiration can come to you from your higher self and there is also inspiration that comes to you from a spiritual aspect. They are similar and yet they are different.

First of all, before we start answering the rest of your question, we need to have an understanding of where we are reaching into for inspiration whether that is within yourself or outside of yourself. As a human being when you come into the physical aspect you bring with you approximately 80% of your spiritual universal energy. The other part of your energy field remains in that higher frequency you can refer to as your higher self or your higher conscience. (Please note this is an average figure, and of course we are all different. If you are someone like Mother Theresa, The Dalai Lama or Nelson Mandela, you are much more aware of who and what you are and so there is more of your spiritual aspect at work. So the more aware or enlightened you are, the higher the percentage of your spiritual nature is coming through.)

When you are seeking inspiration often we naturally tune into that other aspect of ourselves (our higher selves) that remembers who and what we truly are. That part of your reality, if I may call it that, which is universal, understands the choices you made before you came into this lifetime. It enables you to manifest what it is that you need, as it opens you to remembering your real being and what you're predetermined in this lifetime. That is one of the aspects that we are talking about.

The other aspect you can tune in to if you are truly awake and listening can reach into that fountain of knowledge of inspiration from the higher spiritual frequencies to give you guidance in what you need. An example of this type of inspiration of someone tuning in is perhaps best shown in terms of incredible and exceptional teachers and guides, in the gifted musician or artist, in the talented scientist or explorer. When you listen to beautiful music that has been composed by some one like Mozart, which is a good example of inspiration at that level, the energy of a great leader and teacher shows us the right way to be. Christ, Buddha, Mohamed, to name but a few, is also good examples of this type of inspiration.

If you are asking are you on track or doing the right thing. I would ask you Lee to look inside of yourself and connect with your original nature, does it feel right? You already hold that knowing, just tune into it for confirmation.

I feel what we need to connect with is what you pre-determined before you came into this lifetime, rather than go into that other pool of energy. You pre determined to set others paths or patterns in motion in this lifetime for connections with things in a frequency and in an order that you need for your physical experience. I don't mean to be complicating this for you. I am going to say that what you need to do initially is to "tune in" to your higher self or higher knowing to get the inspiration that gives you that "AHA" moment. When you are working or when something is in process you have to make sure that that connection is very clear. Listen to that inner part of yourself to give you direction as to where you are going or when you need to complete or start something. I know for everyone that is not easy, but practice makes perfect. Sometimes it is necessary for someone to visit with a medium to get this insight as their own blocks stop them from doing this. In your case Lee this is not so.

The other pool is so universally vast and it covers so many different plains of existence, I don't want to bring it in too much at this stage. When you talk about your need to start something because you don't want to spend your whole life on the same process I say to you need to follow the processes that you pre determined. Change will happen for nothing ever stays the same, go with the flow and enjoy the journey. Lee it was pre determined that you were to leave your country of origin and come onto the shores of this country which you are now a resident of, for Sophie to be your partner and for you to become a father at this time. Your gift for artistic ability, to be able to see into something with a different perspective than most of us may. That is one of the gifts that you brought into this lifetime. So as long as it brings you joy and gives you what you need I would ask you to honor what the process is rather than cutting it short.

If you find yourself being pulled away from this, and you are feeling uncomfortable, again connect with that energy as a way of re-directing your self back to your original purpose and not being distracted by other things. As I connect with you I am witnessing that there has been a change in the last several weeks in the way that you are working and also in the field and location of where you are working. Within my understanding of that, Lee, this is meant to give you the support that you need. It will not always be that way there will be a time when you have more choice in the decisions that you make and more time to spend as you will.

Your gift is very specialized in many ways for you have pre determined this to bring joy and understanding into other peoples lives. To capture that moment of beauty is something that is very rare. For time moves in your dimension constantly and nothing stays the same for all of it is the energy of change. For you to be able to capture a moment and hold it still is a rare thing to be able to do. With that it brings memory and calmness to people. It helps us remember who and what we were in some other time or moment which we have moved away from. That is very unique in a changing world.

A reminder, when you ask for my input I can not and will not interfere with your free will or your choice of how you go about your work. But I would say as it is unfolding at the moment that you are on track with where you need to be and I ask you to look into yourself and know what you pre-determined how this should be playing out. I would not be afraid to tell you if you were doing wrong, but I would not want to interfere with your karma, it is not my purpose to do that.

I think it is excellent that you are putting your energy into expansion of your work in the way that you have. For it will bring you return which is what you need and there is nothing wrong with you having to do that to make your living. You are here in the physical world partly to do that, to be able to sustain yourself. So manifest as you will, use that incredible creative energy, but when something doesn't feel right then trust your intuition to tell you that it needs to change on some level.

Do not be afraid of the journey as it unfolds. As I say have the knowing that you are moving forward and that you can project what it is that you need to reach your potential, through the knowing of who and what you truly are and why you came here. As I say this, it is also important for me to say to you not to look in only one direction Lee, as trying to reach a certain expectation can stop you seeing what the universe is really bringing you and what journey really is about. So manifest and let the universe bring to you what you need and reach out in the understanding of fine tuning your higher self and your physical self to understand what it needs. I am not sure if I fully answered you question or not. But I will say the manifestation aspect of your work can continue on that road but go with the universal flow and let your intuition connect with your higher self with that higher level of understanding and follow it. Let it take you to where you need to be.

I wish you blessings and blessings with your daughter for she comes into the world in a few weeks. I know that you will be very happy and not to worry about the delivery for it will be as it should be.

In this quiet moment, ask for support and direction so that you may be all that you can be in this journey and radiate your fullest potential out in the world. For the frequency you carry is healing to all of those around you.

Open your heart to receive all the beauteous and bountiful gifts the universe has for you daily. Extend your arms in open posture and just say Yes repeatedly to the many gifts the universe has for you.

Journeying into the sacred Heart is a great exercise, another gift from Jay Paul. Enter into your heart connecting with how it feels today. Place your hand on it if you happen to have a hard time locating it. Many people cut themselves off from feeling because life has become very difficult. My compassion is with you. As you connect breathe into the heart imagining the space between all the cells, the space is a brilliant light, the gold light of the universe. As you breathe let the cells be suspended in the golden light that is there. This is your connection with the universe, your original self. When we have lost this connection we can easily loose our way, feel depressed, sad, and unbalanced. Allow yourself to fully practice being in this space until it becomes second nature, or, I should say, until it becomes your original nature as you walk on the Earth.

Make a collage of dreams and visions a positive focused activity that is tangible.

Thank you God for this offering of love and in deep gratitude, be present to the deep profound thanks for all that is given to you.

Surround yourself with beauty and simplicity, as it is a mirror of who you truly are.

Visual clutter becomes a reflection for us and when we are choosing to see differently what we surround ourselves with is very purposeful. Practice mindfulness when you choose to be surrounded by beauty or the color blue in your room. In doing these exercises you may find the need to change things in your environment, allow yourself to do that, as it is a reflection of your growth and honor that.

Breathe in, acknowledging the breathing in and then experience the breathing out, knowing you are breathing out. With this single minded focus feel the gentleness of the breath moving your body, a wave like motion journeying deeper and deeper into yourself. Allow yourself to enjoy the peace and space, the gentleness and simplicity of this.

Place a hand over your solar plexus and imagine the rays of the sun coming from your hand into your body and enjoy. The rays then travel to the 4, 5, 6, and 7th chakra, out the top of your head to the sun. Let that circuit you have created run, to clear and energize you.

Make sure the tube of listening is clear, the tube that runs outside your body from the solar plexus to the third eye. Connect by touching the solar plexus area then the third eye to stimulate the connection and then imagine traveling down the tube. If it needs cleaning or has an obstacle run an etheric bottle brush through the tube. Then check the clarity of the connection again. Sit in stillness working with the breath. Jay-Paul has taught me these things and it brings clarity to my journey when I do these exercises.

Chapter Six

(In working as a group focusing on global healing we spent some time with the dolphin and whale energies. Their energy is referred to as 5th dimensional frequency. Also as we meditate specifically with Lyn and Jay Paul's CD, "Clear Light Meditation", it brings us to a place of our original nature which in turn is 5th dimensional frequency. It is a frequency of spirit. For when we are in spirit we would never make choices that would cause harm or wasn't of the highest and greatest good for all. If we made choices to cause another person or the Earth harm or discord we would be creating karma from our actions that would need to be balanced somewhere on our journey in this lifetime or the next. We all have a spark of 5th dimensional energy within us. It needs to be awakened within us to evolve.)

Karen: A question came up, Jay Paul, about fifth dimensional frequency and I couldn't answer it.

Jay Paul: Can I have the aspect from the person that was asking this please?

Karen: That was asking it?

Jay Paul: Yes please.

Karen: It was the work we were doing with the water on the map last week. In the meditation I was taking them into the sun coming up on the second day and Mary had asked what fifth dimensional frequency was?

Jay Paul: I will try to explain this as best as I can within your understanding Mary and as also for the group.

Third Dimensional energy what is that?

Let us start off with what you know that is the third dimensional energy. You exist at present in a third dimensional world. Everything around you is at that third dimensional vibration, everything that you can see and touch. It is a physical vibration that allows the laws of cause and effect to be put in motion for time is linear. Past, present and future are all concepts you understand. The past cannot be changed, and the future can only change because of the affects of what you do in the moment, in the now. That is the truth of third dimensional energy.

What is Fifth Dimensional energy?

When we are reaching forward into a different frequency as you call it fifth dimensional energy (lets break this down and rather by calling it frequency let call it a vibration). For all levels that exist in are of a vibrational aspect. Frequency is of your own nature within the vibration. We don't want to confuse the two. Fifth dimensional energy is multi dimensional; time does not exist for past, present and future run parallel. Thought is reality and reality is instantaneous. If you need to experience something it is this vibration: think it and it happens. Process is not part of this dimension.

Fifth dimensional energy is your real home, your spiritual home. Here you can tune in to all aspects of universal knowledge for all doors are open for you to expand into the universal consciousness. You are without form, unless you manifest otherwise, for you are pure energy, light, love and compassion. Density is not part of this reality, for the vibration is too high to sustain lower frequency. Here you make sense of what you have experienced in lower vibrations so you can learn and grow from the experiences of what you manifested into the knowledge of the universal mind.

We have been talking about the changes that are coming into the world with the collective consciousness evolving to be in a higher state of consciousness than at present and in the past (into fifth dimensional energy). For that to manifest fully the energies that inhabit the world need to change their perspective, that is light into darkness. This needs to happen in a different way than how we have been viewing the seasons and how we live. The aim is to move the frequency of the individual so it rises through the third dimensional energy that we presently exist in.

To move into a more refined energy vibration of the fifth dimensional energy. We already hold that higher energy within, but you have to find the key to unlock the door of knowledge, by letting go of the illusion we propel around us and become authentic. If you have the understanding within yourself of projecting your energy into that place of original nature clear light then you are propelling this change because it affects the collective consciousness of your species. Let's simplify this for a moment. When you go inside yourself into a deep meditation or into prayer then you feel your energy physically changing around you. Is that correct? I just want you to hold that as something tangible. You cannot see this change in that moment but you can feel it. Even though the actual world around you stays the same the way you are identifying with it changes.

In some ways moving as a frequency through a dimensional vibration is much like the feeling when you go inside yourself, or when you go to sleep, and even when your spirit leaves your body, either through astral traveling or death. I am going to address this more on a personal level if I may. Please take from what you will and be nonattached to the outcome.

It is about transformation remember again that change is ever happening, it is self-propelling, so transformation is allowing yourself to go with the flow and not fight it. We get stuck when we stand still. Open up to what is going on inside you as an individual, connect with all humanity, all sentient life; this is what you have been and always will carry with you, the memory of all creation. This is what makes up your species and what makes you all so precious. Remember that common theme always, life is valuable and honor it.

If you look upon yourself as that one individual that is able to manifest at least that understanding then you are connecting inside yourself to a greater universal process. If every living human being as you knows it in the world today could do just that process the whole vibrational energy around the world would change.

Does that make sense?

How do we shift to Fifth Dimensional frequency?

The shifting into what we call fifth dimensional energy isn't through war and fear, but through love and compassion. There is going to be a new dawning or a new day. What we are talking about is that more and more of the collective consciousness reaches out into a higher frequency to change how we see ourselves and how we react. How we live our lives. The choices we make.

On a global level it won't change the physical world, as we know it. How we live in it will change our frequency so we can open to a higher dimension on this planet. We will see the world in a different way.

Karen, with reference to "the dawning of a new day", that is a good way of explaining it. For the sun will still rise, the Earth will still be here, but the way we act as a species will change. And the way we interact with each other will change. When the collective conscience becomes stronger more of your original nature comes into being. In other words as I have mentioned this evening to all of you, we won't have to throw around percentages of what our spiritual nature is in ratio to our physical aspect. We will not have to do this for we will be fully awake, fully connected and in tune with our place within the universe. We will still be able to experience a physical life but without the denser energies attacking us. War, famine, disease, viruses, poverty, pain, suffering, anxiety and depression can only manifest in density lower than fifth dimension or vibration. That alone should be enough to want you to make a change for the better.

So the Dalai Lama is an example of fifth dimensional energy, he is awake living in his original nature or truly is his higher self present on Earth.

As I have said if you look at people like the Dalai Lama, Nelson Mandela, Mother Theresa, and the millions of unsung people who are trying to make a difference, you will see they are awake. They have almost 100% of their spiritual nature in their bodies. There is just a tiny frequency that keeps them connected to the universal chain of events around them. They are awake and enlightened so they change the world and the people they come in touch with. If you have ever had the privilege of being in these types of energy fields it is likened to having that universal nature encompassing you. It is like an incredible universal hug. They view the world in a different way. They interact with the world in different way. That is their change of frequency at work. If this can occur on a global scale you can see how this can change the frequency or vibration of everything around you.

Change happens one step at a time

Now this is something, something to share with all of you this process is not a process that is going to happen overnight. It is said in some of your terms that the Earth was created in seven days. The reality of the situation is that nothing changes in that way. Change happens one step at a time. Just as the Earth had to be created and allowed to evolve so that it could support life, so we must allow for the physical impact of change. We are not talking about billions of years in this change of vibrational field in the Earths cycle, we are talking of a handful or so years to come.

Darkest Hour before the Dawn

What is happening in your world at present? You only have to tune into your media, turn on to your technology or read the script that is being written to know that things are happening. You know there are many densities that are playing out their last throws of life in this third dimensional energy field. It is the darkest hour before the dawn.

Old ways are war ways

The old ways, as we would call it, are undermining trying to stop these changes. In denser frequencies, war and disease break out. Suffering is something that is more progressive then healing. What your Earth and species are going through at the moment is an accumulation of thousands upon thousands of years of denser forces playing out. This is why change now has to happen. It has now reached that place of no return, no going backwards. It is said and written in your own text, that those who have got stuck in their belief systems, that have lost their connection to a universal understanding, will and are literally dying for their beliefs within the third dimensional structure. They will not be able to return to Earth energy when we have moved forward. Nothing is destroyed, life always continues, but their energies will go to a place where they can play out without causing any more harm.

Let me give an example. For this frequency to be able to change the individual mind and the whole vibration of the Earth itself, the old ways have to let go. This is happening through various processes, some of them physical in the terms of human beings, but many of them also beyond human control. We have talked about disease and we have talked about war. While those that are willing to die for their convictions seem to cause fighting, pain and suffering to others. These adversities are not going to go away fully until the collective consciousness changes and the frequency of the dimension is increased so that the density sustain hold this frequency.

As you know in your own world in recent years there has been war manifested in different places around you and it seems like war mongers are at play to extend this. I would say to you in my understanding of this that they have chosen to be a catalyst for that in this lifetime, to bring forth the change. Also, have the understanding, that though their understanding at why they are here is not spoken or understood themselves, it is part of the universal process of change.

The new Children are Indigos, what does that mean?

There are children that are coming into this world into this generation and they have been coming in for other generations but more on mass now, which you label as indigo children. I think the understanding is that they are the children of the collective higher consciousness. They are coming in choosing to be more in tune with their higher self and have more of their original nature energy within them.

As the old ways die out, those that cultivate the old ways die out and more of the new energy comes in, change will happen.

Change also happens to the planet as well for it has given itself as an offering to us to exist on, to provide an environment where we can live, grow and reach our potential in human form. The Earth itself has undergone many changes in its creation, as other planets and other places within the universe. For it is natural that things always will change and never stay the same.

With the understanding of yourselves as a species you are responsible for the planet. Understand too, that you have chosen to be re-incarnated at this time, to serve purpose in this change. To bring healing as you understand it and at least bring in a higher perspective a collective consciousness.

Helping the Earth heal is what our purpose is

The Earth itself has been desecrated many times in your history. I am not saying you, as individuals are responsible but as a species, spiritual being having a physical experience, I think it is fair to say that we all should play a part in its healing. Already you see signs again from your text that there are already changes going on around you which are causing shifts around the globe. For even talking of simple things, perhaps like the green house effect or the warming affect, as you call it. That is something that you can see, that is tangible and will be in your face during this lifetime. For it is though the decay of energies such as the pollution and toxicity of the things that are done on the planet are affecting this change in the weather patterns, flooding, drought, cyclones, fires and Earthquakes. Through greed, ignorance, and destruction you have changed the frequencies that sustain you, so the Earth needs to heal from that.

What does the Earth need to heal from?

As a species, you have polluted the land; you have taken the natural resources from the Earth, not to use to enhance the

Earth, but to enhance the physical lifestyle. As a species, you have polluted the waters that give life itself, for land and mass could not exist without the oceans. You as a species have chosen to take thousands upon thousands of other sentient beings on your planet and take them to the brink of extinction. Some of them will never come back and some of them, it is a trial to hold and sustain. As a species, things have been grown in fields in countries and in forests that are toxic not only to the environment but to yourselves. You have chosen as a species to cut down the natural lungs of the Earth as rainforests and from that you have taken from nature that which could cure what is wrong. These are simple analogies for me to make and give to you. But through that process you can see the necessity for the Earth to be able to heal itself through what has been done.

Through the changing of your collective consciousness, through not being afraid or in fear of the manifestations of the energies that play out in the third dimension, you are honoring the change. Let it play out and happen as it will, for over the next few years there will be more and more change in the physical environment, there will be more pollution, there will be more weather patterns that will cause famines, fires, cold spells, hot spells, Earthquakes, volcanic eruptions, some cases tsunamis. I do not wish to bring any of you into a place of fear, but understand that not everyone will perish through this experience This is not an Armageddon as you may have been fed or been given the information about, this is a healing of the Earth.

The Earth has no intention to cause harm to us, as a species, if we talk in sentient terms. The Earth only knows that it needs to heal itself from that which has happened to it. Those of you that are on the Earth in ignorance of the physical reality and its processes, have chosen to disconnect with that spiritual reality of the need for healing, they will not bear these changes well. I am not saying it is going to be easy for anyone. Those that accept change, will not get attached to outcome and therefore suffer less. Those that leave or exit the physical life at this time of change have already pre determined to do that before they even came into this lifetime.

When these energies manifest again into a third dimensional energy for they will, for those energies will need to play out their third dimensional understanding at some time. Their energy will collectively be taken to where it needs to go into another environment similar to third dimensional Earth energy where they can play out what it is that they need to do. For all life continues and is never limited. It is just change. As I have said before, life continues, death is a human concept, one you should not get attached to, as it is an illusion. Energy cannot be destroyed, it can only change.

How, as humans, do we get through this?

And for those of you that will live through this experience as most of you will it is with understanding that you will add something to the Earth's journey and its healing. To reach out to your fellow humanity, to give encouragement and understanding where needed of the philosophy of the universal love and compassion will make this time easier. You have all chosen to be here at this time of change as you have been through other experiences through Earth's changes too. Please do not be afraid of this journey, but honor it, for you have chosen to be here for this purpose.

You are all healers in one prospect or another. You may work in many different ways but that doesn't mean you have nothing to offer. So through this understanding, I hope I have given you a greater context, of the move of that Fifth Dimensional energy than in just feeling it.

If it helps you to understand that all sentient beings through this process (whether they believe or not) they will gradually change what they understand and they will find within them the awareness or the enlightenment they need to be able to propel the world and it's people as a species forward into the understanding of that higher vibration of energy. So that we live our lives here in the future so we can incarnate here to experience the wonders of this physical world, and manifest that totality of our being. So that we are more awake and more aware, and through that journey we will make changes that will be concrete and cemented for eternity. For it will not go back to the old ways. For the Earth will no longer be able to sustain that negative energy because the collective consciousness that we bring to it and that will grow from this it will be something that moves forward and doesn't go backward. This change has been made at this time for many different reasons.

But you all play a part in interpreting your original nature. Even though you may have forgotten it within the human senses there is no coincidence that you are together as a group. There is no coincidence that you are reaching out to a higher understanding of your own abilities and your own potential. For surely it is the understanding that life is eternal it is infinite, you just change and carry on. It should take away any fear you may have in this process. Enable you to reach out to others with that greater understanding, that this is a good journey to be on and not a bad one.

The end to suffering by living in the Compassionate Heart

This is a place where you can choose to suffer no longer in a way that you known. You can bring into your very physical being, into the human heart, that compassionate heart, that is universal. To be more connected so that when you choose re-incarnation again from the higher frequencies you come in with a greater understanding and purpose. To find the joy that this lifetime and many others is suppose to give you. To remove suffering as you know it and to find joy is the very process of being, in human and spiritual terms. To be able to integrate your spiritual energy and your physical energy is a wonderful thing. To be able to live to your full potential and to find the joy that brings you and the happiness and the laughter, the love, the compassion, the understanding, will heal many things within yourselves and your species. That is what we mean by fifth dimensional energy.

So in a lot of ways, it is an internal process which evokes a waking up of the universal process within this understanding. I hope that makes some sense to you. I hope that is something you can think about, to work with and find understanding within your own self, of your place within this change.

You also have the understanding of the blue sapphire Buddha that I give to you, that you are reaching out to others to help them find that place too. You are reaching out to others to help them remove their blocks that stop them from seeing themselves as being eternal. These blocks that keeps your clients in pain and suffering. So your purpose is before you, but it is not **solely** for you. All of you here in the same way share the same processes. It's just that you are the instruments or the vehicles for this energy of healing to come through. This is what you have chosen.

On a sunny day, hold your palm to the nurturing sun and invite it in to every cell of your being. Say yes to it. Then hold it close to your heart as you breathe in its love and support for your journey. Breathe in the sun. With gratitude bless it for it fills your world with love and it the true mother nurturing and creating life.

Hold your hands together feeling the energy that is created and imagine the globe of the Earth is between your hands then ask that the universal healing energies come through you to the Earth for healing. Open your heart to receive and listen then open your mind to be with the Earth.

There came a point in my healing work as a therapist when I was asking how I can serve to the highest and greatest good of all. One day I just knew in my heart that if I healed myself I was healing the Earth. The work with each person that felt drawn to come into my office, I felt the same. I could picture them healed. I was holding that energy and vision in my reality. I knew that if I could create a space for them to heal I was helping the Earth heal. That created peace within me with understanding my work. Clarity and acceptance of my journey went to a new level in my understanding of my work and being of service to others. I heal myself and so I heal the Earth.

I feel the Earth's energies of healing. Acknowledge the vibration of the Earth's movement and with the breath release the energy. For remember we are all energy and light, we can release and move the trapped energy within, therefore, the pain can go as well. Give yourself permission to experience this reality as I have previously mentioned. A great majority of us on this planet have been disempowered to believe we can not heal or shift the pain we endure ourselves. That is a thought that has held us in limitation.

Chapter Seven

The answers are inside you.

I recognize you, Janet.

(Janet asks a question regarding her book.)

Janet: I think my question is something like Lee's and maybe you can't answer it. But -

Jay Paul: I am not trying to get out of answering you Janet, please understand that. Rather I am trying to say that you have already the answers you have pre determined for this journey inside of you. I cannot interfere with that process I can only honor you for it. I ask you to be in touch with your inner nature, your original nature, that higher frequency that we have been talking about, to know that you are on track. I can tell you anything you wish to hear; I can tell you perhaps things that you don't want to hear. What it comes down to is the authenticity of yourselves in your own knowing. That is not something I can tell you. That is something you can only find for yourself. This is what the whole journey is about for you, for your neighbor, for your family, for the town you live in, for the province you live in, the country, for the continent for the globe. It is really all about the same thing. It comes down to how we analyze ourselves and to knowing the higher consciousness you hold and accepting it as part of your reality.

So I am glad Janet that you found the last meeting interesting. I think it is very important to know that although you felt sidetracked, I will say to you that you have to go through your own processes of clearing your own energy and working through your own stuff in this lifetime. Then you can move forward, sooner rather than later. None of us can change what has happened. Yes there is responsibility involved in the future by what happens but we can't change what has happened we can only change the future by the realization of the moment. So there is a process that makes you feel uncomfortable, unwell or whatever it is that any of you feel from one moment to another. Try not to let yourselves get caught up in that energy or feeling because it's so temporary, by the time you have thought about it is past.

Every cell of your body is different one second later to how it was one second ago. Nothing stays the same. So really within your letting go, Janet, you are evolving through this process. It is not so much the mental and physical changes just the acceptance that it has happened. Just leave it behind and move forward. That is the way you open up the compassionate heart. That is the way you feel. That is the way your direction will unfold with your writing and your work. Fundamentally, on a very basic level everything comes down to that which we talk about today, tomorrow, or how we react to a deal with somebody. It all comes down to the authentic intention. You are capable of doing it.

I am not saying that you don't need help, everyone sometimes needs help. You may require prescription medication, sometimes you may require alternative healing practices, and there is not one of you here that has not experienced one or the other of those things. They are tools to help. The driving force behind you as spiritual beings is you're original intention. What do you want to manifest? What it is you wish to project to reach your potential? Remember that life is a process, not an exercise that is instantaneous. Allow yourself to heal in that and move forward.

So Janet, in terms of bringing it back from the generalization to you individually, your spirit is very much awake. Your physical aspect of understanding that you are reaching out more strongly, just allow it to come in and to flow naturally, for when it connects it gives us the ability to heal ourselves all the aspects of our being. Does that make sense to you?

Janet: Yes, it does.

Jay Paul: You're more than welcome my dear and I am pleased with your progress. You are doing very well and for those that help you too.

For personal healing

Use Rose Quartz crystal as the mineral vibration of unconditional love to absorb any pain which is energy and send it to the furthest reaches of the universe where it will be transformed. Release the energies into the quartz and give gratitude and thanks for this. Sometimes we need to invoke our unseen friends to hold extra energies for us to do this. I remember lying on my bed with a strong voice demanding help. In the moment the pain shifted. It was amazing and empowering for me.

Creating a personal vortex

Place your hands in the stance where you are sending energy with your right hand and holding or receiving with your left hand. Your intention is to ask that you create a personal vortex of energy in your energy field that will serve you to harmonize and balance all your systems and provide you with universal healing energy on a constant flow until otherwise notified. . As you sit with this experience allow your heart to be open to receive, listen and open your mind to the images, colors, feelings you may experience.

Direct Vortexes- At an area of vulnerability in your body create a smaller vortex asking the universal healings energies to balance and heal the area. This vortex may serve as a protection or a buffer as it will continually supply healing energy until it is no longer needed.

Chapter Eight

Getting stuck in the process or lost is a human condition.

Janet: Can we get stuck or lost in the process?

Jay Paul: Absolutely, to get stuck or lost is a human condition. That is how Karma the law of cause and effect evolves. You predetermine certain aspects for your spiritual growth and for your universal contribution. So when you predetermine something and it doesn't work out properly, you have then in all likelihood used your freewill and changed this into a series of events that will take you on a totally different journey. A karmic journey you would call it.

A Karmic Journey

With the choice of using your free will, it is a karmic journey.. For example, if you were to get cancer and you found some wonderful way to hold the cancer in check so that it didn't take you from this lifetime for 20 years, it would be because you had pre determined to live that way, for that extra 20 years with the burden of the disease rather than without it. So what I am saying to you that there are certain things that are set. There are certain other things that are not so firmly set. The gift that you bring into a lifetime is always pre determined. You can enhance what you bring in to a lifetime, but the very nature of the gift as you may call it, is something to help you live a more full life and to help others around you also share that understanding.

You have an understanding in this physical life that contracts have to be made in spiritual life for certain circumstances to evolve. This is done on a universal level, a soul group level, an energy level, where certain people have to be in certain places for certain events to unfold. So people will come into your life, when they are meant to.

Now, if you had pre determined for example that you were going to work in a certain situation using your gifts and that you were going to meet somebody who would perhaps be your teacher. A situation like that, I also feel you would set in stone, because the contracts have to be met. What wouldn't be set in stone necessarily is how you would use your gift. That is your freewill that is your karma.

If you used your gift, to manifest a positive cycle in your life and other people's lives, then your contract would be adhered to. If you use your free will and choose to use it in a negative way the impact will be different. Both variables are subject to the law of cause and effect. The choices we make can carry forward from one lifetime to another lifetime if out contract hasn't been completed or fulfilled, as it was meant too. Not the things set in stone but the things around freewill and how you use them.

Part of why Universal Law does not interfere with your freewill is because it is through the learning process of not following through on the contract, or not fulfilling it in the way you pre-determined, that becomes your greatest learning curve. For those events, that are negative in your life, are what we learn the most from, and unfortunately these events, hurt us most. These are the experiences that we learn through; it is with the understanding that we should bless those negative events because they are your greatest teachers.

Can we ever be perfect?

Now, if you were to come here and experience everything through your original nature, from a place of non-attachment, you would be very blessed and regarded very highly. You would be tuned in with this aspect of yourself that would be similar to that fifth dimensional frequency of energy which we have been talking about.

I think this is another process even to add on to Mary's process for all things are interconnected. When we are in physical form in third dimensional energy we often do make our freewill choices in a negative way. Not because we are really choosing to do that but through our own ignorance of being disconnected to our true self. So the learning journey takes you the long way around and probably through many lifetimes to sort one thing out from another. This is something you will see changing around you as the changes around us happen.

One of the things to be aware of in this life time, in this time frame, which I will limit this discussion to because I am not linear myself, that karma, as you know it or the law of cause and effect, is only something that is manifested in this third dimensional frequency that you live in. You have to take responsibility for your energy, for your life times, your direction and guidance. But the coming of this change in the universal understanding means that all this karma, these energies need to be balanced from the third dimension during this lifetime rather than over many. That is why it is so necessary now for the Earth to heal itself too because once this energy changes, once we connect completely with ourselves, karma, the law of cause and effect, will not be the same as you know it now. That higher understanding, that the higher fifth dimensional vibration won't sustain energies that drive karma, as you know it.

The nature of being in the physical world will still be limited but you won't be making those negative decisions in the same way that has propelled in the third dimension, because you won't be ignorant of your choices. You will have a higher understanding a higher consciousness that will make you more spiritually, emotionally and physically aware of something before you do it. I hope you can understand this.

I want you to discuss this at some other time within the group on a more generalized scale. It's like turning off the tap and starting a new pipe system. The energies are changing and you won't be taking your information from the same source as the tap. You will be connected with a totally different system, the water will no longer be polluted, and the water will be fresh. We are talking here in metaphors.

Universal colors

I am all the colors of the rainbow. Allow the breath to take you deeper into that understanding. Be present and take notice of any images, pictures, colors, feelings that you may have, as each of us receives and processes our messages in a clairaudient, clairsentient or visual medium.

The journey is discovering how you perceive.

Chapter Nine

Wake up; Open up to channeling energy in a new way.

Karen: Do you see this fifth dimensional change of frequency happening in our lifetime?

J.P.: Yes. That is why you have chosen to be here in this lifetime, as the change happens. I am not saying that everyone here present will experience it but as a generalization most of you will, yes. And you will awaken to that part of yourself you have been searching for most of your lifetime in this present physical environment. You will awaken to your original nature. You will not be able to stand still, because the reality of your existence will change. You will find that within this awakening, if you will call it that, through this process of change that the way you react in the world will be very different to how it has been in the past. Those who cannot sustain that understanding or that reality will have predetermined to exit this Earth before this happens.

Although it may seem now to be complicated it is also something that is realistic. As these changes propel themselves and the Earth changes propel themselves, the more your consciousness wakes up, you will open up. As a species, you will channel energy in a different way.

How much do we channel now?

At the moment you are only using such a tiny part of your own mental projection and consciousness. So tiny that you won't even grasp at this stage what awakening really means or reaching into yourself for that enlightenment. But it is a process that will kick in strongly. We have all come into this world at this time because of these changes. There are those people that suffer greatly and have many problems. At the moment, they are playing out their third dimensional roles and trying to make sense of things. They are often overwhelmed from a physical and psychological standpoint.

You have all preprogrammed yourselves for want of a better way of putting it, pre-determined to be here and to be awoken as this process comes in. So your consciousness, your mental ability, and your physically body will know it. It will open up as this awareness comes in. You have chosen, to be, for want of a better way of putting it, asleep for this time. When that other reality opens up you will wake up and it will flow naturally. Don't get caught up in the process of how this will actually happen, and what is going to happen. Let the universe bring it to you. Just as you pre-determined it will. If you can get into that quiet place inside yourself, if you can connect with that universal part of yourself, you will gradually open up to that understanding without any fear. That is why it is good to meet in groups like this. It is good to meditate because it brings calmness to the storm as it were.

Practice Mindfulness

In meditation stance, focus on your breath. Follow the pathway as it travels through your body, as it feeds and nourishes you consistently. If you have feelings acknowledge them as you breathe in and smile at them as you breathe out transforming them into a lighter frequency so you are clear to open your heart. For example, as I breathe in I feel the anger inside me, as I breathe out I smile on my friend anger once again. As I breathe in I feel my heart racing, as I breathe out I smile to my racing heart. Work with this in the next 5 minutes to center yourself and to bring yourself into the present moment.

Now that you are there, look at the picture, acknowledging the way it makes you feel. See if you can project yourself into this beautiful place. Allow yourself to sit beside me on the rocks or find your own place to be. Open your heart to listen and feel the senses this invokes.

Frequently, allow yourself to journey here. Each time it may take you deeper. Open yourself to that reality.

As you progress along, for healing you can add as I breathe in, I am the mountain as I breathe out, I am solid. Thich Nhat Hanh describes beautifully this positive imagery to invoke the strength and knowingness within us, that calmness to be in the truth of the moment, to see clearly and lovingly with compassion to others who are struggling.

Practice Mindfulness, is choosing to be consciously aware of all our actions, our choices, in thought, in our daily lives, at all times, in the present moment.

Chapter Ten

Patti asks a question around illusion and reality.

JP: I think I am going to label this the difference between perception and reality rather than illusion and reality. Common condition in the human understanding is that we are all raised in a physical environment, where we are taught to look at things in a certain way. So our perception of things is different perhaps to the original nature of things. That is the best way I can put it.

Original nature

A very basic example of this is what I have often used is - if you look at a glass of water, you see a glass of water for you to drink, to nourish your body for that is something that you need. But your perception is to think of it as nothing more than a glass of water. If you look at it through the illusion of the perception, at its original nature, you see water in the glass that has been part of the ocean, that has been part of your atmosphere, that has been nurturing something before it even has come into your glass. If you look at the glass you know it has been made of fire and sand at the loving hands of somebody who cares. So you are looking at the same thing and seeing different things. The physical projection of energy, as I can best put it to you, is that you see what you want to see, what you have been conditioned to see and no further. That is very third dimensional in nature.

How can we exercise changing our perceptions?

With practice of removing the illusion and seeing from a place of clear light, or our original nature, we can really see what we feel an object to be, because some part in you in another reality is waking up. If you were to stand now as you are in a forest of old growth trees you wouldn't just see the wood. You would see the life that formed that originally. Part of you is waking up to that reality. When you are with another sentient life form and I will bring trees into this category for they have a life pulse of their own. You would feel the heartbeat of the tree in your hand now. You would be able to wrap your arms around the tree and feel its very energy source. But at one time in your life you couldn't do that. Open your heart and you will see a new world.

Change is hard, but try this is your experiences and grow in the learning and knowledge of this new view of life, for it will bring many different levels of joy to your heart and mind. When we connect more fully, with our higher aspect of fifth dimensional energy, or that original nature, you will automatically see into everything what reality really is, rather than third dimensional ways of perceiving it for its use, as a glass, and nothing more. Within this understanding, if you look at the Earth itself, when you look at the Earth as an individual, you have more compassion and love for it. It is literally your "Mother Earth", a sentient being.

I know with Lyn's experiences if she is to turn on your technology or read the script that shows the pain and suffering she finds and identifies within herself the bases of unhappiness and suffering. For she feels the pain of what she sees written down in the pages or the pictures that project the suffering. Initially that suffering can hold her. She can be working, as you have, with somebody that is sick or somebody that is stuck somewhere or grieving, it is easy to be pulled into that field. To perceive it as exactly what you are seeing as somebody else suffering. Lyn has had to learn the hard way to move the illusion and to understand that our suffering is also our liberation. It does not mean that she does not care, for indeed she does, but it means she can have more to give if she is not attached to the outcome.

There is so much pain!

If you think of the analogy of someone turning on your television set or reading the paper and you are reading about the biggest explosion that has just happened in Iraq or wherever it maybe in your world. You are just seeing a manifestation of that very physical energy in a horrific way. It is not the way the universe really intended it, because it is third dimensional energy playing out negatively. If you look through the perception, the illusion, and you see what you have here, are beings that have chosen to experience this as some part of fundamental growth in their universal understanding. The playing out of karma perhaps or what it is they need to play out in these horrendous conditions gives you the courage to give unconditional love and compassion to those that suffer. To understand the nature of suffering, to understand why there is a need for change in the universal aspect then you are seeing something that you still may not be totally comfortable with but you are seeing a picture that makes sense rather than just a perception. You can then approach this with love and not fear.

Seeing with Fifth Dimensional knowing

I often liken the circumstances you are experiencing in third dimensional energy as though you are looking at a picture of a beautiful world but are caught up in this tiny little space on the edge of that world, caught up in our own reality, as we perceive it what is happening. The difference between doing that in third dimensional energy would be like looking at the same picture from being awaken at fifth dimensional energy is that you see the whole purpose of why this bit is playing out and not just being caught in it. From a higher frequency you also see more clearly the whole picture, of what is manifesting and evolving, not just the part you are caught up in. So there is validation in your question within that understanding. But as I say, how it plays out differently in third dimensional to fifth dimensional energy it is the unveiling of the illusion the perception.

Affirmations

I am the light, I live in the light, I love the light, and I am protected, supported and provided for by the light. I bless the light.

I am god, I am Buddha, I am Narayani, Divine Mother of the Universe, I am Archangel Michael, I am Mother Mary, I am.... (Use any ascended masters or light beings that resonate with you)

It is all an illusion. This is an illusion. Look at the world around you and acknowledge that it is an illusion. Look at something specific and say it is an illusion. Pain is an illusion. It is all an illusion.

As an exercise, sit with a flowering plant that is not flowering at the time. See it as having flowers know with your heart that the flowers are within this beautiful plant. Send it loving and compassionate energy holding the focus of the flowers. You may notice within a week the flowers will start to come. I have done this several times with violets, my jasmine plant and the wonderful Christmas cactus. If your plant is not healthy spent some time with it and look deeply as to what the cause maybe. It may want to be moved, put in sunlight for the afternoon or watered. They are sentient beings that are cohabitating with you. Honor them for that.

Reveal yourself and trust that god lives within you and every breath you take, for you are god and god is you and you are one. Your mind and the godheads mind are one. The understanding that you share is profound and like a beacon transforms others on their journey to opening their hearts to the truth. For the truth spoken in any form or language is the truth for its frequency is truth.

Thich Nhat Hanh has two beautiful books that helped me with healing my wounded perceptions: "Anger" and "No Fear, No Death".

Chapter Eleven

Guides or guardian angels

Jay-Paul: Is there anyone else who would ask me a question? I was going to come to my friend here on my left for I felt his energy hovering here, for a few moments.

Willy: I have been spending some time reading Kiron and I have a new guide. I am asking for clarification. I know that my guide has changed.

JP: "The truth is the truth". We have many roads to find them. Ashara is your secondary guide's name. In my house there are many mansions – quotes Christ.

Willy: Thank you.

Jay-Paul: You're welcome.

Can you explain some more with regards to guides and guardian angels that are with us to help.

Jay-Paul: Perhaps if I can help you with a little insight.

You mentioned that your guides were changing. What I want to say to you, is that your connection that you have with your universal energy, there is one always that stands with you and acts as guardian to you, and that doesn't change. For it is of universal purpose. There are other secondary guides or energies or whatever you wish to call them that change frequently pending on the need that you are having. The understanding you have with your caretaker energy, your guardian angel, however you wish to think of it, it is something that is pre-determined through the life time. We call that your Gate Keeper Guide. They are not necessarily experts in all aspects of being but they chose to walk the path with you and keep you constant when you need them. They are your best friend, your helper, your angel.

Why do secondary guides come in to help us?

Often what propel us are other energies to come in. On a universe level, they have experienced different things; they come in to help you during changes. Even in spirit we are all interconnected. We reach for higher understanding and knowledge no matter what our stage of being is. Look upon them as different teachers, if you will, they are experts in certain areas of your life or what you are doing or what is happening or unfolding in your journey. Know always who ever is with you, that they are here to help and to guide with the understanding of unconditional love and compassion. It is not their job to judge, only to support and help.

Within your understanding of things changing around you, Willy be open to the new concepts and ideas that manifest universal love and support, guidance and knowledge. Those that work with you will change just like you were in school and moving from grade to grade your teacher will change from time to time, but the principal remains the same. Does that make sense?

Willy: Yes, it sure does.

Jay-Paul: I want to talk to you about what happens between life times. My process with you is to help you reach the understanding of the reality or bardo or plain of existence in this higher vibration without physical form.

Energy as I say does not stop. It manifests in many different ways. This is so true as you move between the space between physical life times, in different directions or vibrations as you progress. It is as though you are part of a thread of understanding that you have gained from your physical experiences that you weave into the universal fabric of understanding. And that part of you that is attached to whatever you call it, spirit, or universal energy, is irrelevant because you are, and you exist, that is all that matters. But in that place you go through different experiences, you go through different realities; you initially face your fears perhaps because of the need to balance an effect you have caused. You are given plenty of opportunity to work through those things and then you find your dreams and make those happen, as it were in your life. You propel the energies so you can make them happen.

Within that understanding you are in a place if you want to put it in physical terms where you can tune into that universal university, that library of knowledge, that thread of energy, which exists however you wish to interpret it, where you can learn more information all the time. Where you can integrate that aspect of what you have experienced to what already exists. You can then with your guide make the choice of returning to the physical world or not.

Universal University

So even in between your physical experiences in different life times, you and your guides are all are going through the process of learning at a universal level. Information is manifesting around you and into you. Learning and the change of our teachers and our guides in the process of life that we go through, is just like everything else it is never-ending and always changing. I don't want you just to think it is learning through the physical aspect because you learn also between lives. You are part of an incredible universe. Your very nature is to grow in knowledge that is constant. Does that make sense?

Karen: Yes.

JP: I'm glad. For if it didn't I would not serve any purpose.

(There is a lot of laughter and the group is opening up.)

Chapter Twelve

Pregnancy

Karen: Sophie wanted to know if she was going to give birth naturally.

JP: Well I think it has already been said to you. If you don't mind me saying so, everything will be fine. Please do not be in fear of this. I know we say it is harder to be born than it is to pass over or to die. You have no memory of your coming into this lifetime as your baby will have no memory of being born also. Can I just say to you that in that understanding I see that it unfolding in a perfectly normal natural way. If you need to take anything to help sustain you or help you there is nothing wrong in that for all things exists for that purpose. Please do not be in fear of the outcome you will produce a healthy baby girl. That is what you pre-determined. There is much joy there.

Lee: I have a question for my wife as well?

JP: For your wife, can she not speak for herself? - I just jest with you!

Lee: There is a concern about her spiritual growth now because she says she doesn't feel much now.

JP: I feel I do not want friction in your understandings here, can I just say that the nature of being pregnant, is the nature to giving birth, the nature of expectation. The energies can't be everywhere and scattered for she could not give to herself what she needs to for the birth of her baby and this experience she has chosen. Sophie, in relation to that please don't feel you are lacking in that for you are experiencing just what you need to from a universal perspective. Everything that you experience and do at the moment is just perfect for what you need. If coming to these talks and sharing helps you on your journey then that is enough. But it is meant at this moment for your energy to be focused on what you are going through.

Sometime in the future in a different reality to where you are now, you may serve purpose by remembering some of things that we have discussed coming more into alignment with them as you unfold and grow in that aspect. But now you're unfolding and growing as the aspect of becoming a mother literally and that is fine. So do not worry about that aspect, and for you Lee, do not worry on her behalf about that because all things work for purpose as they are meant to. Let me share with you that the knowledge of your baby has heard every word that has been said. So not only is this a process for you. So nothing is wasted that is what I am saying. Just serving purpose as it is meant to. We are honored to have you both here and your baby this evening and that the other times that you have come.

The Children in our lives are precious and sacred.

Our children are also our greatest teachers, for they will reflect what we need to heal within ourselves.

In the Indigos, their knowing is complete for they hold the energy of the future, the fifth dimensional frequency we all have lying dormant within us. Some of us that have awoken to that remembering work with those children supporting their energy and purpose. Very often they know what they need. Encourage them to join your breathing or meditations and ask them what they see. What colors you present to them as you journey into the clear light together. Ask your child to teach you to remember the truth. Honor them for their journey for being in a world that does not support their frequency for it is a difficult one.

There is a deep knowing within them that they will be taken care of, a frustration at the lack of justice monetarily distributed on the globe. I remember my daughter always saying everyone should have the same. There is enough. Money shouldn't be the way we live with each other. Innately she was expressing the old frequency needed to shift. They are also great in manifesting so team up with them to help them manifest what your dreams are together. By asking them to teach you, you empower them. Empowering them makes the light within them grow brighter, so they can be all that they can in this lifetime. For they have great purpose.

When we consciously choose destruction and pain for others we add to our karma. In this 5th dimensional understanding karma does not exist. Making the choice to harm or cause pain will be unthinkable. We will choose harmony and balance for ourselves and for the planet.

Support with love our children's journey for it may seem uneasy, as they are a minority on the Earth planet now. A day will come when they will be of majority holding that frequency so love and peace will prevail.

Chapter Thirteen

Closing blessing

Lyn's energy is starting to tire somewhat so if there is no further questions I will take my leave. I thank you for allowing this to happen, for giving me the energy to help manifest this.

Please know that I am no different from you for you are me and I am you, we are all connected for we are all part the same universe. You serve purpose and direction from where you are. You add to what I add to, what I am in your experiences I add to what you are and all of yours. Thank you for sharing and being here.

I hope this has helped you in some way with some of the things that were perplexing you.

I asked that you move forward from tonight and always live your life with the understanding of being spiritual beings, not just physical and to be able to project what you need to manifest so that you can reach your potential.

You each hold that key within yourself; do not be afraid to unlock it.

I wish you well on your journey and I know we will connect again.

In the meantime, I ask that the light of the universe always be with you.

We took a few moments in silence as Lyn came back into her physical form. The group then broke for refreshments.

Part Two

Healing of the Mother Earth
Global Issues

Chapter One

It just so happened I was invited to spend Christmas season with Lyn and her husband. Aly, Angel, our feline companion and I drove out to Lyn's small town, in one of the most inspirational valleys through the Canadian Rockies.

Christmas Eve, Lyn wasn't feeling very well she was picking up the energy of a wave of destruction. She asked me to get her a world map so she could show me more clearly what she was feeling. Her energy was drawn to the Indian Ocean. We would not know for a couple more days the events that would unfold. We decided to do some work clearing and re balancing her energies. This resulted in me afterwards writing down some information she was receiving on the Earth and some of its changes for 2005. I like to refer to them as insights. They are available on her website www.lyninglis.com.

On Christmas morning, my daughter, who is quite sensitive, woke up feeling sad. We thought it was pre adolescent behavior and told her it was Christmas and there was no need to be sad. Our Christmas day was that morning the Tsunami happened in Southeast Asia.

On Boxing Day, we then heard from guests that were visiting about the devastation. I went to retrieve my emails and found one from classmates of Ally's on a world tour that were in Phuket, Thailand. The email was a first hand sharing of the disaster. It brought the whole experience of the event closer to home for us.

The following day, Lyn and I knew we had some work to do with Jay Paul. Sitting in her office, looking out on the beautiful snow lined mountains with the sun shining Jay Paul's energy entered with warm hellos for the beautiful sunlit world we live in.

It was important that he share the universal perspective on the Earth changes, globalization, and the need for humanity to come together to support each other with love and compassion in amongst the wars already at play. He also covered how we need to think differently with regards to the drama around oil, of what he terms, as the blood of the dinosaurs and the destruction of that age, and the oils' energetic effect on humanity. Specifically, he also shares with us where and whom he works with around the world.

I had a huge awakening and learning with regards to his message around the Star Wars concept. We talked about its possible repercussions for life outside of our planet.

We discuss energy in the cosmos and it ignited the remembrance for me that I am a spiritual being made of light and energy having a physical experience. The physical limitation that we have come to play out in should be our only limitation to express with freedom fully who we are. The energies of control and power that we have created as humanity needs to change so we can all be free with the same rights to everything. That control and power have become additional limitations that were not intended by spirit.

Open your heart and your mind to listen with all of who you are to experience the words expressed by Jay Paul around these urgent topics.

He also leads us through some beautiful imagery or some would call it meditations. Give yourself permission to experience with your whole being.

Breathe in, knowing you are breathing in, then breathe out, knowing you are breathing out. An exercise Thich Nhat Hanh teaches in all of his texts. For the breath is a miracle, it serves life. Again, breathe in, gather that mental energy, or thoughts, and exhale.

With love, I give you Jay Paul.

Chapter Two

Dear Jay Paul, many of us are feeling angry, lost and questioning if there is a compassionate god and how, if there is, could these Earth atrocities and devastation be happening. There are so many storms, mudslides, Earthquakes, hurricanes that are resulting in many of humanity dying. Can you shed some light of understanding on these questions especially around the tsunami?

Let's start at a place on this Earth where this immense disruption of energy is happening. Most of the world does have the understanding that sometimes these things happen and a normal part of the natural movement of the Earth's surfaces. In the case of these larger activities please understanding that what you are experiencing is of the Earth's needing to heal itself rather than the Earth's need to destroy. As I have mentioned the Earth is a sentient being in its own right. The Earth's gift to you is one of love, for it is a place of beauty. A planet like this, in your understanding of the cosmos, is a very rare treasure.

Many of the things you are experiencing are the fallout of cause and effect, especially where the weather systems are concerned. I will give you more details as we speak. Perhaps though, I can put this into another perspective, which you will understand. Within your own body sometimes you can be vulnerable to sickness and pain. This is sometimes something you may have gotten because your body has been infected with a bacteria or virus. When it can your body will use its immune system to fight. Or for example, if someone were to violate your body, you would have to go through a process of cleansing and healing. This really isn't any different to the Earth itself.

When we talk about the Law of Karma, the cause and effect of things, I think it is important to point out this happens only as a result of energies playing out in the physical world. It is not something that relates to the higher frequency and dimensions, the higher planes of existence. However, Karma is measured by the forces of the laws of cause and effect in the physical world with some impact into the frequencies that are higher. Before you incarnate back into the physical world a large part of your choices are around what you need to experience and what you need to balance so that you can grow in love and compassion.

You understand that we, as souls, are all the same age; I have never liked the idea of young souls and old souls as you are aware, but rather prefer the term as related to the "experience" of souls. The more experienced a soul is the more understanding, hopefully, that they will gain in the physical aspect of their journey. So the repercussions of karma in the physical world, to those souls who are more experienced, shall we say, are higher in universal terms than for those souls that are not so experienced. For example, if we take the journey of the man who is inexperienced in the physical realms and he creates different densities by choices there. He will have to come back and balance that energy in the physical world but the repercussions of it aren't so great as it would be for a more experienced soul, who chooses density. This soul, who has more experience, should know better. In some ways, you can look upon this as a web that has been woven. The waft is not so fine on the inexperienced one and much finer on the experienced level. So there is more impact on that fine woven cloth than there is on the cloth that is coarser. Does that make sense?

Karen: Absolutely.

Jay Paul: Yet, it is also agreed upon that those souls that take the hardest journey are usually those that are more experienced. Not because they wish to create more density but there journey is more challenging. I am not suggesting that there are people that are suffering through the cause and effect of what is happening on the Earth at this moment that has asked that this is part of their karma. But they would have had an understanding that their exit in this life would be from some natural catastrophe. This is perhaps dharma at work, the experience or learning. Karma is in effect working more with those who have survived than those that have passed. There are going to be many millions of lives in that part of the world whose journeys are going to be affected over the next weeks, months and even years. It has affected millions of people.

There is Karma for they have to re build. Karma is not instigation for those that have left during this but for those that survive it. They are having now to start the processes of finding the ones they love that are no longer with them, their bodies have washed ashore. Homes have been destroyed. The infrastructure in some of the cities and towns has been destroyed. The flooding, the seawater has mixed with fresh water that is rare and there is a propensity for disease to break out such as cholera and typhus, as you are aware and other water born diseases such as malaria. There is also a propensity for infection such as dysentery so they have a lot to live through and have nothing there to balance it with.

You mentioned this yourself yesterday, Karen, it is though the carpet has been pulled out from under their feet and the ground itself and can no longer be trusted. So they are Karma that is living, for they now have choices in front of them when they are over the worst of the grief they will have to start rebuilding their lives from nothing. The karma is measured by what they do next rather than what has happened. I see that humanity will open its heart and help in a way they have not done before. You are opening up to help others that is good, that is what is needed.

Why does this happen to the poorest countries?

Jay Paul: Things happen in different ways in different areas. I will say that there are many that go to these continents and lands that choose to do so to strengthen their spirits, they are very brave souls. As I have mentioned previously, the hardest journeys are often chosen by more experienced souls. These energies have chosen to experience many things in a very short period of time. The density and the mass is part of the choice that they make to belong to and to experience these things on that level. Their growth potential is incredible and this is why I say Dharma plays a part for it is now what they do with the situation that makes good or bad karma. Keep in mind that it is with the universal understanding that the Earth has not meant to cause harm but only to heal it self.

*This is an urgent message to get our act together
as humanity.*

This is a wake up call as much as anything, an understanding of the need to reach out as a species. There is a need of understanding that we are all here to help each other. Eventually, as more of these things happening in the world, over the next couple of years or so, the overall reality is that man will wake up to that understanding of interconnection.

There is sadness within myself, within the understanding of the universe, that humanity has to manifest in this way but there is no other wake up call that has not been tried. It is the destruction that is happening around the world and natural causes that will draw people together rather than pull them apart. The strength that will come out of this, the rebuilding of life as it should be rather than how it has become will be what moves your species forward. Already, you can see that humanity is reaching out in a way that it would not have done, if this disaster had been propelled by war, race or creed etc.

Karen: Thank you for that clarity.

After the Earthquake in South Asia there were waves of intense fear that traveled around the Earth. There was also the joy that followed the release as well. Bless the energy that was expressed by the Earth and all sentient life forms so that it may serve in the cleansing and healing rather than to cause destruction.

JP: Realize too that in this sequence of events that man is not the only one that is affected for much in nature has been affected too.

Journeying into the sacred Heart is a great meditation, a gift from Jay Paul through Lyn. Let us take this moment to be in that quiet space. Enter into your heart connecting with how it feels today. Place your hand on it if you happen to have a hard time locating it. Many people cut themselves off from feeling because life has become very difficult. My compassion is with you. As you connect breathe into the heart imagining the space between all the cells, the space is a brilliant light, the gold light of the universe. As you breathe let the cells be suspended in the golden light. This is your connection with the universe, your original self. When we have lost this connection we can easily loose our way, feel depressed, sad, and unbalanced. Allow yourself to fully practice being in this space until it becomes second nature or I should say until it becomes your original nature as you walk on the Earth.

Breathe in, acknowledging the breathing in, and then experience the breathing out, knowing you are breathing out. With this single minded focus feel the gentleness of the breath moving your body, a wave like motion journeying deeper and deeper into yourself. Allow yourself to enjoy the peace and space, the gentleness and simplicity of this.

In this quiet moment, ask for support and direction so that you may be all that you can be in this journey and radiate your fullest potential out in the world. For the frequency you carry is healing to all of those around you.

Hold your hands together feeling the energy that is created and imagine the globe of the Earth is between your hands. Then ask that the universal healing energies come through you to the Earth for healing. Open your heart to receive, and listen, then open your mind to be with the Earth.

Chapter Three

*So much money has been spent on war and space projects
the focus seems out of balance compared to the poverty,
famine and disease in our world.*

Continuation of the Tsunami discussion

JP: The purpose of the west and of the eastern role in this.
The monies that have been spent on control and power in the
world could have prevented all this from happening. It is said
for those that live in the West much of their karma has been
good, for most share a privileged life. Shouldn't that give the
people that hold the power an advantage to change your
world into a better place? There is enough in this world for
everyone to be fully sustained, and disease free. The 2004
Tsunami is a wake up call for everyone to reach into their
humanity, to reconnect with who they really are and
remember we are all connected, so reach out to help. When
disasters of this type happen they often occur in places in the
world where there have been hostilities, pollution and
overcrowding.

Karen: Where the energies need to be re-balanced.

JP: That is correct. This is one of the most densely populated
areas of the Planet. So, it is a clearing of pollution on some
levels. The natural infrastructure has been removed and
being replaced by buildings for those who would travel with
money, to be able to lie on the beaches and I am not saying
the world does not deserve that, but people go to places
where children are starving, where there's begging, sickness,
where there is abuse for many and they sit beside this and
they don't understand the compassionate sharing of
humanity.

What you have said is overwhelming and true.
What is the solution?

There needs to be more sharing and caring. There needs to be more understanding of the spiritual values of connecting and being connected. So you will see Karen unfolding in front of you as you go on through your life with more understanding of that. It is just unfortunate that these series of events had to come out of karma to bring that understanding out to all of mankind. Yet there are those that still, do not see this, and will take advantage of those that are so vulnerable. Please realize this is not some divine plan made by the Universe, rather it is the effect of energies playing out as they need to within the physical Third Dimension. Always the universe is compassionate and loving. There is no joy at what is happening. The message for everyone is: As a species, you are responsible for your actions and this Karma is what is playing out.

Karen: When I look at the globe I think of Iran, Iraq and the Middle East, it is not very far away.

JP: The energies are so unsettled in the Middle East. That is why many great teachers have come to and lived in that area to try and bring peace and understanding. The energies there are perhaps some of the denser energies in the world. At the same time, great light has also been experienced there. It seems to be the place where energies play out against each other. Tribes have split from their original families. They have forgotten that they share the same roots, which is their common humanity. Politics, religion and greed have severed that connection. Yet still, there are many living there that are compassionate, loving and wise. We pray that their light shines and brings peace; That their love will overcome fear; That their common humanity will come together to move forward so that those around them can all reach their greatest potential as loving compassionate beings. There are two forces at play in the World, love and fear, and only one can win.

Where do you foresee the next place of impact?

The next big impact will be in the central Americas coming out of Mexico. Mexico City will suffer some damage and the lands south of Mexico will be susceptible to quakes in the next year. There is also the propensity of tsunamis in that area of the pacific moving towards Hawaii. There will be some activity in Iran and still in Indonesia. All around your world quakes happen thousands of times each year that you are not aware of because they are too small. The Earth is changing all the time. These smaller ones are part of the Earth's life cycle. The larger ones however are the devastating ones. These are partly a result of the balancing of energies due to humanity's misuse of the Earth's gift. If you could all live in harmony, as you are meant too, then there would be less of this type of activity. Lyn mentioned that she could feel the rise of energy coming from the south moving north when this devastating quake and tsunami happened. The energy that will happen next will move in a central location, move south rather than the north, so there is a balance.

We have to keep life in balance as much as we can. That is part of the understanding in the holding of our personal energy.

As we anchor in these higher frequencies to support our new direction it will augment our thoughts and choices.

If I am too busy, how can beauty and peace make itself known to me? If your busy-ness becomes a distraction in life the awareness has already come to you to ask the question, why am I creating this? The active lifestyle then becomes an obstacle or avoidance of something. Honor that, be honest and truthful with yourself and journey with the breath into understanding your choices.

There are many blocks in the third dimension, which n we have created to keep us from the truth: distractions, addictive behavior, poisons and the ego. In this moment, if you can ask for the authentic intention in this moment to let these obstacles, go for the highest and greatest good of all, let it be so.

I am a single mother and I am self employed and was going through a time where my love for red wine was a passion. I started to realize that I wasn't sleeping well at night. Because of this my attention was off and there were days where I felt sick for most of the following day. I knew for my highest good I needed to let it go. I didn't feel strong enough to do it by myself. I asked for my guides and the angelic realm to work with me to help me curb these experiences. I knew it wasn't serving me. It took me over 6 months floating in and out until now I can say that I will have a glass and sometimes it will just taste awful or yummy. When it tastes yummy, I will sit back and enjoy the glass of wine. When it doesn't, I will throw it down the sink and feel okay with that knowing it is for my highest good. I also know in my heart I have set up that system with my guides and honor it.

Slowing ourselves down to be patient and take the time to perceive things in their original nature, rather, than how we have been taught to see them will start to shift our reality and lift the veil of illusion. For example, looking at a glass of water we can conclude that is a glass of water for the purpose of quenching my thirst. Now take the time to truly see that this is a beautiful glass made from sand heated from loving hands and filled with water that once was in the cloud as rain from the ocean. Then the experience of drinking the water becomes different. A reverence or an appreciation for the gifts we receive from Mother Nature and this planet giving thanks for this nourishment. We need to create the patience and space to embrace this interconnected understanding of all things.

Chapter Four

Who is Jay Paul and what does he do in our world?

Karen: Thank you. I know Lyn had mentioned to the group that you come through a couple of hundred other people. Who are those other people? It was a question I have asked myself. As I was searching the net, different sites came up and I would read something and I felt, Oh boy that feels like the same resonance as you, as I speak with you. I feel that is a way the universe answers me is by giving me those pieces and I just ask for guidance around that.

The other part was the multi dimensional and parallel universes. Very often, I feel with various relationships, certain people are familiar energies. I know I have a connection with them but it feels like a connection on another plane of existence or another dimension. Also, it doesn't feel that it needs to be played out in this reality. It is in my opening or waking up to those different concepts or feelings that these messages are coming in these ways.

JP: (Smiling sweetly) so which of these questions would you like me to answer first?

Karen: We can do the first one first.

Jay Paul: I work with various people. I say 'I' because it is something you can identify with. However, the reality is my energy is made up of millions of spiritual energies that have evolved into this universal understanding, so that we can share with you. Lyn knows me as Jay Paul, but others know me by other names. What is more relevant rather than a name is the energy we work with. For we do all we can for the highest good of universal understanding only. When we manifest and work through different individuals, these individuals are connected to this group of energy through their own frequency. It is with the understanding that this information can only be channeled through a frequency that is open to receive and will share this knowledge. That is predetermined before an individual incarnates to your Earth.

I am known by many names. We come through with the understanding of the highest level of being that you can relate to in a physical world. I said to you before that the essence that comes from my understanding or the understanding of all that is a melding, if you like, a coming home of the collective consciousness of millions upon millions of essences of spiritual energy that have evolved to this understanding. Some call me Michael and I am also known as the essence of Darwakll. But the level of understanding of the consciousness that we reach into is vast and I do not want to limit it to one existence.

We have been male and female; saint and sinner; great and small. We have been all things; for we are all things. As part of the collective consciousness of life, we have all worked through darkness to become light, and by doing some have awoken to our original nature unconditional love and compassion. That is why we reach out to you, to give you direction to find you the way home to the same unconditional love and compassion.

We come through and work with those on the Earth plane that have some level of understanding obviously not as great for it is limited in a spiritual sense when we are on Earth. But to those that are a little more awake we work in various countries. We work with various individuals and with groups to help bring knowledge and light and understanding as love.

Let us look what is going on in the world, their purpose is, at the moment to make some sense of this. Let us go to what is happening in the Ukraine and the breaking out of the dissident population of honesty and truth, to get rid of the density of the government or those that take part in corruption. Dissidence in this sense is good. It is positive. I work with the process of many people that came together as a group for the understanding of the highest level of humanity: the freedom of choice and truth. So within that understanding we work with many individuals in a small group so that they had the strength to stand up to what was right, even though these horrific events have happened. Even though we see someone who is now their leader, who should be dead, we gave him the strength to do what he came here to do. That is one example.

China

If we cross your globe, the government in China is starting to change. I am not saying it is near where it needs to be. We all have to start somewhere, and at least now it is lending an ear to the understanding of freedom of rights and is giving more choice to its people. We are working in the knowledge that this energy will soon manifest itself into giving insight into government and politics so that they in turn will work compassionately with those living in Tibet and Taiwan. To open in freedom and understanding to create peace and joy for these two countries without fear, so that all peoples can benefit. It is not always necessary to work as an individual but as part of a greater consciousness.

United Nations

Perhaps in relation to individual rights I want to move back into your history into the 1950's where from the darkness of war came the opportunity and need for a greater understanding and unity. The United Nations was and is the manifestation of energy from this source. Specific individuals have been brought together to work as a collective to improve everyday life and give better human rights for individuals, and their countries. To bring into being the words and actions, truths and strengths, that is used to make this world a better place. When we work together in harmony, for the benefit of humanity, and not just for individual governments or individual leaders, then we move forward, making a far more tolerant world for all sentient beings. The results being, that we evolve as spiritual beings having a physical experience. We bring universal law into our daily understanding. We have freedom of thought and expression to become all that we are.

One of the conflicts that is happening in the present is that you have the American government working against this energy of the United Nations. When in the physical dimension, we all have the right to defend ourselves. War is never something that pertains to the common good. America has backtracked and has moved away and gone on its own defensive. Resulting in a process where they do not have full control of what is happening around them. I am not by any means just pointing my finger at one country.

Rather, I am saying there is, in truth, no difference between the two sides. The ruling force between both sides is very similar, neither wants to lose, and both want to win. They both want control of the outcome, no matter what excuses they use. Both sides are manifesting the energy and destruction that is presently happening. They both have forgotten their place within the world and failed to understand the value of humanity. So we work within the structure of bringing people together, as best we can. We work in understanding that it is better to work with groups such as, The United Nations. Ultimately, they work for humanity and not their own ends.

Argentina, Chile

We also work in the continents of the Americas, both south and north. Where there have been civilizations that have come and gone, where in the past empires have invaded and taken away the very substance of living and peoples have suffered. Now the energy is moving, slowly but surely towards light.

In many other countries, such as, Argentina and Chile, there was much cruelty, people went missing, and there were many atrocities committed against man and his environment. Humanity, at last, is waking up to the need to end destroying ourselves and our environment. Globally, Native Peoples are waking up to their rights and their freedom. You can all live in harmony, in peace; you just have to have the authentic intention to do it.

Africa

In Central Africa this destruction is still playing out. In the Congo, Rwanda and The Ivory Coast just to name a few places, we see terrible unrest and the need for light to quell the darkness. Yet, if we travel a few thousand miles to the south, wonderful positive energy has been allowed to manifest. It represents itself in many ways, as Nelson Mandela and Desmond Tutu to name just a couple of wonderful souls. Yet there are many unsung heroes too. They are awake. They have the insight to turn adversity into opportunity for peace and joy, love and compassion. They have been able to turn the destruction of Apartheid around and it has happened with peace without more death occurring. The people have overcome the atrocities that have happened and now treat each other as equals.

Love and compassion can over come all things, just allow it to flow. I know there is much poverty and disease still in this area, but again humanity is coming together to overcome this. Density is the frequency that allows disease and viruses to manifest. When we bring light into that frequency of destruction, over time we will see these terrible things disappear. For all those that are reaching out to express the love of humanity, know it is not in vain. You are much honored.

Chapter Five

Listening

If we travel to other oceans and cultures there is an understanding in the world to stop, and to listen, and breathe a while, that is good. I have mentioned some of the other countries in the southern oceans where you have been in the Hawaiian Islands, south of where Lemuria existed there have been times in your history where there have been those who used terrible explosives to pollute and destroy. That doesn't happen anymore.

There is peace there now, although you yourself could still pick up the destructive energy associated with war. It is possible for areas of land to still hold the aura, or energy, of an experience. That is what you felt when you were in Maui and that is what the Earth still feels. This is why the Earth needs to heal itself.

Gradually, the Fifth Dimensional energy that I have talked about with you in the group is in all of you, but it has to be opened. Sometimes we have to experience devastation in our lives for that energy to open. Sometimes we have to witness atrocities, and sometimes we have to feel that pain ourselves. We are fighting against a wall of third dimensional density that would hold us in a negative place, if it could. We have to remove that wall in front of us for our own Fifth Dimensional energy to open up. All these incidents that I have talked about and all the people that bring light into the darkness are trying to help broaden the understanding of universal love and compassion.

This is a process of waking up. Horrendous, though it may seem. On a universal scale there is an understanding that bad and good experiences happen. For we have to experience all things on our journey. We have to know darkness to know light. The journey is about moving forward, but in understanding and experiencing the darkness, we grow in compassion and that adds to our greater spiritual understanding. I don't want to take anything from those that have had bad experiences, but know too, that in universal terms, they are a mere flicker of an eyelid, in the existence of spirit.

As spiritual beings you have experienced these things yourselves many times, that is why we are here now, to bring the experience of our universal knowing into human form, to help the world and humanity through these changes. We then have compassion in our hearts so that we are open to those who are going through similar circumstances.

Prayer for Humanity

We ask that those who leave this world are not too traumatized by the experience, and waken, and move into the light with ease. Knowing that what they have chosen to experience is to add to their, and the universe's growth. Also, for those that are here and now on the Earth, we ask for guidance and light to be sent to all those who need help, so that they may grow strong from their experiences and are then able to move on in their lives with open hearts, and so that they can connect more fully within their fifth dimensional energy. We also ask for those who are in power to work with positive and good energy and to open their hearts to the universal truth of being and not limit themselves by the desire for power and greed. We ask that they find joy and love and share it. You literally hold the future of your world and humanity in your hands.

There is enough in your world for everybody to sustain themselves so that they can give their energies to their true being and open up to their potential. For this to happen all voices need to be strong, all truths need to be heard, for us to practice unconditional love and compassion so that our spirits can soar. A voice does not need to be stopped or imprisoned for voicing truth through speech and the practice of free will. Things are starting to change. This is what will eventually allow you to reach your potential.

When we are talking about these things, whether it is from my understanding, from the group, or the universal truth, it goes into any heart that is open to receive it. It cannot be altered, the truth of existence cannot be altered or covered up, there is no division to those who are sick or to those that have died, it does not work like that in reality. Fifth dimensional energy needs to flow freely. The Earth healing itself is the breaking down of this third dimensional energy or density.

Listening to what the Earth is saying

Let us open up to that inner strength of knowing that we are universal.

If we live in harmony and peace we hear that the Earth needs to move itself and move to safe places. If we can all listen with that fifth dimensional energy we will all know when the Earth needs to heal itself, whether that is by a flood or famine, whether that is by an Earthquake or a volcanic eruption, we would be able to hear the Earth itself and know. For as beings we can chose to avoid these situations, and come back to the places once they have healed. Part of the

Fifth dimensional energy is learning to hear the needs of the Earth.

At the time of the Tsunami, December 26, 2004, Lyn heard or felt a bit of the Earth's healing call. She may have not fully understood it, but she had perhaps 24 hours notice that something was going very wrong. If we all listen as humanity to the Earth's healing message, we could stop the present suffering and decrease future suffering. That is why it is important to reach out to individuals and teach them.

The idea of the development group is to teach these individuals to listen. Just to confirm, the fifth dimensional hearing is beyond the physical boundaries as we know them. That is what waking up means. Obtaining enlightenment, or awareness, is irrelevant if you can't hear the Earth, if you can't see the Earth.

I am going to bring this into a different level with you Karen, There is a reason that your connection with sea mammals is so spiritually important. They exist in the same fifth dimensional energy you connect with. Their sonar systems pick up earth events before they happen. They stay away because they live that energy and know it is not a good place. Even though they swim under the waves and currents and are not affected they still move away.

Karen: Allowing the Earth that space to shift.

JP: That is correct. It is because they listen. Human beings have a lot to learn from the animal species. It is known, for example, before an Earthquake or volcanic eruption the birds fly away, the animals move to safe ground while they can. They listen to the Earth. They might not know what is going to happen but they have generations built in to that energy system that tells them there is danger and they need to move away.

We have to listen to that as humanity. We have to remember that we have this same ability. I am not saying that we can avoid every situation but as we open up to the 5th dimensional energy more of us will hear "that is not a good place to be today". And we will be able to remove ourselves from that location so that the Earth can do what it needs to do. Then the rebuilding can start again. But although these events are still catastrophic in their consequences, development they need not be totally annihilating. Does that make sense?

Karen: Oh yes.

Why don't we listen?

JP: In Lemuria, Karen, in your own history, those that knew the Earth change was coming either chose to stay or moved away. You knew it was coming so you went on your journey towards Tibet.

In Atlantis, some knew it was coming and moved to Central America or Africa and some chose to stay, and those that did, chose to exit their lifetime in that way.

Karen: You mean the ones that chose to stay?

JP: Yes, but not all the ones that chose to stay knew what was to happen. There were many that didn't know what was happening, perished because they couldn't hear. They hadn't awakened. Their minds were filled with technology concentrating on machinery of control and war. How can you listen when that is the focus of your mind?

Karen: Yes.

JP: Yes, there are places in the world that are deaf. They do not hear, because they have so much that their mindset is pulled by which is totally irrelevant to their real purpose

Karen: Like a distraction.

JP: Absolutely

The Big Ear

JP: So when you work and use your energies, when you are working in the development groups, or your lectures, or the courses that you will be offering in the future, the basis is to clear all the junk. Physical and emotional so you can feel the Fifth Dimensional Energies. Once those are part of your very being you can interpret them with clarity. This is why this exists, the energy field here between your third and sixth charka that is your inner spiritual ear. That is why it needs to be understood and kept clear.

Karen: That is one big ear. (Laughter)

JP: (laughter) that's a big ear. This is where you feel things.

Karen: So much of humanity has cut that off because it has become so painful.

JP: It has become so painful, or they have been distracted by fear: Fear of war; fear of what someone else may do to them even though it maybe totally irrelevant and it isn't going to happen; Fear that they may loose their home or their jobs, or the clothes on their back, fear that they don't have the biggest and best house, or car, or whatever it is. Most of humanity is tuned into that fear frequency.

Karen: They don't listen. How can they listen?

JP: That is one reason, in this lifetime, you and Lyn, for example, and those that will be working with you will choose or have chosen to live in this hemisphere where perhaps fear and greed is the densest.

Karen: That is what I find in the development groups. My purpose is to help heal that resistant energy of fear and self doubt before people can hear.

JP: In the physical terms it is like removing the wax from the ears. (Laughter)

Karen: Absolutely.

JP: Or the blinders from the eyes, or the wall from the solar plexus. That is why we work with developing peoples senses, so that they have the need to connect not just with spirit, but with the world around them. That might bring a different aspect to the work with the development group, if it's put like that. As well, being fuel for more words to be sent out into the world in publication as a script.

Create the space to create change. See yourself stepping back, out of yourself, to let go.

As we anchor in Fifth Dimensional frequencies to support our new direction these will augment our thoughts and choices in the positive change occurring before us.

Chapter Six

Creating space for compassion

How do we find this space within our hearts where we have compassion and listen? How do we clear the tube that is connected ethereally to our senses, so that we can be part of the experience without having to suffer? It is by growing and learning. It is by growing through the causation and coming to terms with cessation and understanding that is what opens that.

We all have a responsibility to help each other wake up.

That is what I want in the book Karen, all those events and aspects in and of our world, those things that stop us from waking up.

View the view from the window, open the door and enjoy. I say when those doors and windows are closed to spirit and those who suffer the karmic implications are strongest with those that have the most, because those that have the most have walked a long journey to get here to this place and should know better.

Those that suffer the Earth changes in these places, the karma open the opportunity for them to grow and to move in purpose and to build strong karma for them in the physical sense. For us, that just watch, if we do nothing to help people wake up then the implications of karma are stronger because we have already walked that path and should know better.

Fear versus Love: Why is fear so strong?

We should have learnt from that experience but ½ of your population in your western world comes from a place of fear rather than love. That is what needs to be changed. For sometimes we have to go through grief and pain to find love. We don't have to destroy everything in our sight to stop that process from happening.

Trust the universal energies supporting your journey for it is precious, sacred and you are honored for it.

All my needs are abundantly met now and forever. All my needs are abundantly met now and forever. I accept good graciously in my life. All my needs are abundantly met now and forever. It is so. It is so. It is so.

As you breathe in and know you are breathing in, then breathe out and know you are breathing out, as Thich Nat Hanh refers to is, the Buddhist way it brings you into the present moment which is made up of the past and holds the unfolding of the future. So being in this present moment is where heaven on Earth lives and where life is. Nurturing the seeds of happiness and ceasing the nurturing of the not so happy seeds will bring forth an awakened mind, which is an aware mind. Mindfulness is the blood to go deeper into knowing. Being peaceful and calm allows the moon or sun of truth to reflect so the truth can be revealed.

When emotional seeds are watered, such as anger or jealousy, be like a mother nurture them with love and compassion and they will transform. I am that....I am... We can be in a place of choosing which seeds we will nurture.

Open your heart to come into communion with the energy you are embracing. Breathe into the moment knowing you are breathing in with them in harmony. Breathing out knowing you are breathing out in harmony feeling the energies merge and dance in celebration.

Chapter Seven

Fuel of Life

There is so much fighting with wars over oil. Why the greed and poverty, lack of sharing, the wealth is only for so few looking at the world's population?

Presently, the wealthiest people are the war mongers. But they are only wealthy in the physical sense. Spiritually they are totally disconnected; their karmic implications will be very strong. For as I say they live privilege lives and have used it to manifest wealth at the destruction of life itself. The oil that they take from the ground to fuel their wealth helps many in the western world and the whole world be able to travel, to be able to have a better standard of living. I am not saying that that is wrong.

My title of this chapter is "Fuel of Life"; I purposely choose this because within your global realization I want to bring in another variable that needs to be fully addressed to help change the frequency of the density on the Earth. The majority of fuel that is used for all purposes comes from the Earth itself. More importantly, from my understanding; is to give you some knowledge of why some things are playing out as they are.

For this we need to address the use of fossil fuels. Without becoming too technical, the want to take you back in time millions of your years ago when dinosaurs were the dominant species on your planet. This was a time when life was based on the dominance of the strongest of species. This certainly was not the time when spiritual growth had any real impact.

This stage was certainly an important part of the evolution on your planet and the Earth provided the environment for the forming of basic life forms. As you are aware from your scientists, life at this stage evolved much on the reptilian level. Even within your physical form you do have that part of your brain that has a reptilian nature. The experience to understand life at the level of fight or light was necessary; and this period of time life existed in your world for many millions of years. It is quite a feat for nature, the seeds for which were planted by universal growth and knowledge.

This was a time of survival of the fittest. It was a time of the biggest and most violent creatures in nature. The energy on the Earth at this time was extremely dense, to be able to support this. When the Earth itself was threatened by this density the age of the dinosaur became extinct. The universe itself provided the necessary energies to end this stage of being. Again, this is universal law of cause and effect working.

Your known history shows you that over time a very short period of time Earths environment started to change and it could no longer sustain itself. The ecosystem transformed itself for the next stage of development of sentient life. The atmosphere changed, the forests and wetlands that had once sustained these life forms disappeared. The multitude of bones of the dinosaurs literally sunk into bogs; and then over millions of years turned into what we now use as fossil fuel.

I do not want to make this any more complicated that it needs to be. But the density of those millions of years and the process of nature allowed for the growth of these "dead" forms to turn into the fuel you use today. So, the basic elements that drive your world come from a place that has been propelled from a very negative density of experience. That aura has never changed even as it has been buried for millions of years.

103

Oil and fossil fuels are the basis for most of your economy. Wars are fought for ownership of these fuels rights, density is manifesting in your environment and atmosphere from the use of these fuels. The aura of these fuels manifest is greed, control, ownership and war in your world now, perhaps more than anything else. If you put these facts together, you will see why the world is also partly in the mess it is. How can you reasonably be able to construct a healthy world that is not polluted literally from the ashes ad the bones of that past environment? I want this to be food for thought.

There is much in your environment that can be used to manifest and harness all that you need without taking from an age of death and decay. Why have you become dinosaurs of greed when you can become angels of light? Everything has been provided for you from the flow of universal energy and its interaction with nature, you have been given all that you need to sustain yourselves and your eco systems in harmony and balance with the Earth. Teach your children that it is not necessary to rape the Earth of its minerals and chemicals which are now the building blocks of your environment. Teach them to listen to the Earth. Teach them to become one with the universe in how they grow and understand life.

We are spiritual beings not these physical dinosaurs that have long gone. There is everything to sustain us in a way that we don't have to take from the resources of a species, whether sentient or not, that has been long dead. It is not necessary for our economy and wealth to b e based on such an ancient dense energy as fossil fuel.

If we open up to that Fifth Dimensional energy and make contact with the universe itself, which is within all of us, we will be given everything for the answers already exist. The answers for survival, travel, pleasure and to live in a ecologically supportive way that is not reliant on negative, decayed material, all needs to be balanced and in harmony.

The Earth does not have to be raped and civilizations lost. History doesn't have to be raped for us to move forward.

Let us change our focus for a moment. It is beautiful to hold a crystal and manifest it to help us. As you have read through your own words, as you have read through many experiences, Crystal Mountains already exist. They offer themselves to us, so we don't have to rape them to get what we need.

Please understand, we can only move forward as a species if we stop taking from the Earth that which is gone. For how can we grow in understanding to utilize this free energy, if we take the blood of the past to nourish the future?

We need to take the energy of Universal Spirit to propel us forward which is our given birth right. We do not need to take from anything that has existed before, but only for what is there for us. I offer you this as a different perspective.

I want to bring to your attention in helping people to think, making people realize they can manifest what they need without having to take unnecessarily. In your history you laugh about something being a dinosaur or decayed, and yet you take its blood and its fossils fuel. Is that appropriate for a world that is opening up? But what is more inappropriate is those resources have made the destructors wealthy and users- the rest of the world- poor.

Karen: Using fossil fuels has caused war, anger and greed.

JP: Precisely, because that is what that pre-historic age was all about.

Karen: The dinosaurs held that energy.

JP: Yes, that is how they existed. For that energy, life force had to be experienced to create all things, but when it was no longer appropriate, it no longer exists. For we can give, and we can take, but only as is appropriate.

Karen: So by using the blood of the dinosaurs, this oil to propel our vehicles or to heat our homes, we are bringing forth this resonance, that frequency of greed and destruction. Oh my goodness.

JP: Precisely. Remember too that this oil, and things manufactured from oil and similar resources is what is polluting most of the world today. Look at the "Green House Effect", and the pollution in your atmosphere and in your oceans.

Karen: The thousands of oil spills affecting the mammals and the birds. It is killing us.

JP: Precisely. When I am talking about death, I am talking about in a physical sense, the third dimensional sense, not a spiritual sense, you understand that?

Karen: Yes.

JP: Spiritually, life is everlasting in that sense. Physically, It is impossible to have only good come out of that density. That is why war usually comes to those that take that type of wealth. As you say, that is why where there is fossil fuel; the very energies that sustain your world in balance are being melted away or undermined by the dense energy. The Earth's reaction to that is the cause of events that are happening now.

The Universal Perspective

Karen, for our book it is important to bring an understanding as to the "why" rather than just the "how". From our viewpoint in spirit we can see the beginning of existence, the whole picture, rather than the physical illusion of today.

You have now reached that point in time where something has to change because you cannot move backwards anymore.

The universe is compassionate and living. It wants to give you the chance to recreate your world, to propel the planet forward and its own evolution, for the highest good. We ask for life to grow and flourish in the best of ways. For we have chosen that the Earth has given itself to us for that purpose. When we take from that darker density, we receive at that darker density. The opposite effect is, we receive in light and give in light. That is the highest truth of how humanity should be, then the natural balance of life is in harmony.

New ways of thinking

JP: Within those terms, we need a whole new way of thinking. The energy for that thought process is already within those that come into this lifetime as Indigo Children.

For those that are reaching out to grow, you may not hold the technology to build an incredible windmill, but you can support the ideas that are of integrity in this new direction. You can support moving forward and stopping the things of the past and the things that are negative, you can choose how you run your home, how you run your cars, or vehicles, you can make those decisions as an individual. You can too make global changes if you are open to working together to make a difference for the better.

Negative energy attracts Negative energy

If you go back into history to the time of the Nazi invasions into other countries or back into the time when they were trying to find heavy water in Norway to create atomic energy. They were trying to divide something that naturally exists in nature, to destroy humanity on a large scale. The creation of atomic energy in its time and nuclear power was initially for destructive purpose.

Now, while there is still the problem of weapons of mass destruction, it would appear there many benefits also. This is an illusion. When it goes wrong, and accidents do happen, it causes destruction. The Chernobyl melt down occurred in your lifetime as an example of what can happen.

Look at the pollution of the seas from nuclear waste and atomic waste. Look at how that is affecting indigenous life. See how polluting energy and fall out going into the atmosphere spreading not just a mile here and there but is carried with the clouds in your atmosphere surrounding your planet destroying the natural ozone levels and the air that you breathe. This is another cause and effect in motion as this too causes disease.

Humanity is messing about with things that they know very little about for the purpose not of the highest good. It literally is a time bomb.

Heal the wounded perspective and projections we create. Thich Nhat Hahn's books are fabulous for working with this concept. Two I can think of that helped me were "Anger" and "No Fear, No Death".

What you would term your greatest enemy could be your greatest teacher in teaching you life lessons. I have always felt that I had big learning ahead when I sensed a sea of negativity approaching.

Since the beginning, I have felt my mother has been my biggest teacher. Allowing me to journey into the conscious purpose of that awareness was important for my personal growth. I know that she was there so I could choose differently around what love is in my life how it expresses itself and that thought is a powerful essence to our well being.

Thought, I truly believe, if it could be seen or tangible would be like seeing Pig Pen on "Charlie Brown" walking around with the murky fog surrounding him visible to us all. Thought is energy and choosing to think positive brings in the higher vibrations rather than the lower frequencies as we have explored through healing resistant energy.

Gregg Braden "Returning to Zero Point The Collective Initiation" and some of his other books has done research around the vibration of love, as opposed to hate, love lights up more strands of our DNA when it was tested. I found that fascinating. There are huge healing attributes to cleaning up our thoughts and choosing the lighter, brighter, loving dialogue in our heads. Yes I can, I think I can, no, I know I can.

Wishing our greatest teachers, such as our mothers, loving kindness, on a daily basis will transform them, or the situation; it maybe an effort but is definitely worth a try.

Hold the space to choose differently, work with the vastness and expansiveness of our being. In the Clear Light Meditation or working with the image of the sun is a start. Embrace yourself beyond the vastness of who you are, like the rays of the sun extending outwards in all directions. .

Plant the seed of intention that these meditations serve for the highest and greatest good of all sentient beings.

Using intention augments and shapes our meditation with clarity for the direction of energy we are creating. .

Start allowing yourselves to bless everything that comes into your path or enters your consciousness. For example, bless the highway as it gets you to work, bless the bird that thought of poverty, or struggle, bless that thought of joy, bless the coffee, bless the chocolate, bless the Soya milk, etc. Allow yourself to be creative, see how things start to change.

Keep pure thoughts by listening to music or singing mantras.

For example, the Dalai Lama always starts his day with, Ohm mane pad me ohm. Robert Thurman's book "Circling the Sacred Mountain" has a fabulous dissertation on the meaning of that mantra.

Try playing music that calms or clears like the sound of the Tibetan bowl or Ohm chanting is great to quickly shift the energies in your office or home. These techniques clear the resistant energies.

Chapter Eight

This time bomb you refer to, will it explode or can we do something to help ourselves and the planet?

Jay-Paul: On the positive side people are waking up to that. It is now the 'dinosaurs' of certain countries that use that type of energy. They need to move forward. They need to learn in here (pointing to Lyn's heart). They need to listen from here, (as he touches Lyn's heart). They need to see from their hearts to be able to manufacture what is harmless to the world. That will give us what we need.

Let me give you an example of a different way of using your own energies. Karen, in your previous existence as a Tibetan monk, you have known, and experienced, tantric exercises where you have practiced out in the cold Himalayan winter where you were wrapped in wet blankets and have dried them within a few minutes by using your own body heat. You learnt this through the concentration of energy. We all have within us, the power to do these things. You had learnt to listen. You learnt to deal and hold other higher frequency of energy so that you could do that exercise, as a means of survival.

As a species, if you could remember all this knowledge you hold within you, you would manifest what you need and wouldn't take what isn't yours.

I am not going to spend any more time on this for now. I want to bring that reality forward for thought in a way that can be put into a book form for others to understand their choices and how it affects all around them. I don't think people as a generalization, think in terms of what they are using and getting from the Earth as having a cause and effect on all sentient beings.

Karen: I don't think so.

JP: Of course the need for war, greed and control exists, because humanity has forgotten it already has everything it needs. Society has evolved so that you have given your power away to those that would control you. This is something that currently that needs to be understood.

So I feel there is title for you out of this much information for you. (Laughter)

Karen: I think so (Laughter)

Chapter Nine

Closing

JP: I think it is time to call it for a rest for a few hours and we will continue this later today or tomorrow it is to do with your own choice.

Karen: It is just a question of driving home safely in the winter weather. I felt guided by Red Hawk either to leave tomorrow or Wednesday, pending on the weather.

JP: You will be safe in getting home but you want to leave before the snow returns.

Karen: That's right and whether that is Tuesday or Wednesday do you have any feeling around that? I can have another day here.

JP: I think we could serve good purpose if we were to continue in the moment, if you would wish to if that would make your decision easier for you?

Karen: Let us come back together this afternoon. I will get Lyn and myself some lunch.

JP: That is fine.

I would like to share the physical sensations when I am with the purity of spirit. Jay Paul for me holds the space so I can remember my original nature. It is powerful and beautiful, compassionate and transforming.

When I am sitting with him and he is journeying for example around the globe to the various places he works with as individuals or groups, I travel spiritually with him. The energy is all encompassing and like a cushion we come to a place of communion with each others energy and I am in another place.

I physically am still sitting in the chair facing Lyn's physical form but the energetic coming together of Jay Paul and myself, make it a shared experience.

It is like going to a rock concert where there are a lot of people, huge frequencies of music pumping through speakers, which in turn resonates through my whole body. When I leave the concert all my senses are heightened, alive and buzzing. When I walk away from the forum and start to "come down" as some would say, I notice that I am either hungry or thirsty. The needs of my physical body become a reality. It is like I could have been in that space of music for hours not moving, just being transported to a place of experience. Walking away from the concert I am no longer in that space, so reality, the walking away for example, to the car, begins to ground me. That is what it is like for me in session with Jay Paul. I hope that has brought you some clarity and tangibility.

As we completed the discussion and broke the connection of energy, walking downstairs to the kitchen, I realized how hungry I was. I also felt tired. I knew nourishing myself and drinking some water would bring me back to balance. Lyn and I sat and ate profiteroles with ganache, cream puffed pastry with a rich creamy chocolate sauce. It was Christmas, after all. We also turned on the television to the news to see what had happening in Southeast Asia.

Part Three

Star Wars
Universal Issues

I will share an interesting comment Jay Paul made before we began. When he re-entered Lyn's physical body for our next discussion, he asked me what the heaviness in this area was, pointing to Lyn's stomach. I told him, Lyn and I had eaten some profiteroles and chocolate at lunch. He commented "Oh, some decadence," I hope that made you smile.

With love, I give you Jay Paul.

Chapter One

Globalization

With all of these changes happening around you, I feel a propensity to talk about some changes in the infrastructure from a political standpoint rather from a geographical situation. This regards globalization. There needs to be an understanding of political unity, whether that involves economy, politics, or government.

In this higher frequency and dimension, that I speak to you from, it is understood that everything that occurs on your plane of existence is universal rather than just global. It is not only limited to your physical world.

As the Earth moves into its future, and as you evolve as a species, this will manifest in some changes of the physical environment. As the negative energy changes into more a more positive frequency, (third dimensional environment that goes into the 5th dimensional environment), it is worth giving some deliberation, as to how things will unfold.

It is important to remember that you share in a common humanity. You need to plan to put events into effect so that things can move forward in harmony with compassion and understanding. In doing this, the experience of change can be put to good use.

The dynamics of the Third Dimension are very limited. The sense of survival is very basic, that is why negative energy continues to limit the understanding that we are all one.

Again, if you remember you are spiritual beings, not just physical, then it will make your choices much easier. Individual countries are fighting for their status amongst many other nations. Even amongst their own traditions, there are conflicts and divisions between political, secular, religious and ethnic groups.

As a species, and also as spiritual beings, there needs to be an infusion of understanding so that bigotry becomes something of the past. Even within your own energy systems, in your lifetime, there have been conflicts within many countries resulting in a breaking down of communities with different backgrounds and belief systems.

If our politicians and our leaders, whether spiritual or secular, could come together to bring changes in your global understanding of what humanity really stands for, then you can move forward without being so limited in choices. You would no longer have to live by politics, dogma, creed or fear. The barriers need to be lifted; your common bonds need to be honored.

In a spiritual reality there is no distinction between any forms of life, for all is precious. All on Earth are precious too, that is why we are always reminding you of love and compassion.

The Need for Freedom

Freedom of choice is also worth mentioning. Only through freedom to choose can the spirit manifest what it needs to fulfill its Earthly destiny. Now, I am not saying that the knowledge of extreme limitation when communism, fascism, bigotry and hate have been at play has been wasted because to understand freedom you have to experience limitation. However, enough is enough. How many times do you have go through this process?

The Need for Unity

From a universal perspective, being in the third dimension gives you enough restrictions for your spirit to learn what it needs, without other restrictions put on it. It is time, in your frequency for change. Globalization does not mean the loss of your individual traditions; rather it provides the opportunity of honoring them.

There needs to be unity. The understanding that your biggest birth right as spirit, coming into third dimension frequency, is to have freedom of physical, emotional and spiritual expression, with these, you are able to explore your potential.

This is the message your leaders need to understand. They should be chosen for their humanity, not their power; for their compassion, not for control; for unity, not for separation.

Our True Purpose

Again, the true purpose, if we go back to when the physical world was created, was with the understanding of providing a wonderful beautiful physical environment for spirit to come into and experience itself, in a limited frequency.

The journey into density is to find the light within and then to return to your original nature through the process of changing frequencies at death. In physical reality, you get to experience things very differently than in the higher dimensions.

The Earth is an eco-environment given that has been given to you to try and sustain sentient life. There you can feel and touch, love and hate, have joy and sadness, all the extremes of physical understanding.

The journey of life should provide you with those experiences which allow you to gain a greater understanding of compassion and unconditional love. So that you can return to spirit with the joy of knowing you can overcome all obstacles and have an understanding of universal law at work in limited frequency. This is how you add to the growth of the universal mind, for we are all one.

What is it like in Spirit?

In the higher vibrations, for example, if you were to create the most beautiful flower it would become part of you. You would know it, as if it was a part of you. In the physical world, it would be something that is separate from you, yet you get to physically hold and cherish the seed that then grows into something beautiful. You can touch it, smell it, it is a very sensual thing.

Karen: It is a tactile experience.

J.P.: Third dimensional experience is to use your senses to be in touch with them in a way that you cannot do so in spirit. For as I have said many times, Reality and thought are instantaneous, in spirit. So thought produces reality. In the physical world, events have to be put in place to manifest within the framework of time and space.

You all need to take responsibility to be able to grow and to nurture yourself, both on a physical and spiritual level. Just as you need to look after yourselves, you also need to be able to take the land, the dry Earth, nourish it with water, sow your seeds and have an abundant harvest.

Chapter Two

Human's Psyche's Need to Control is Not of Spirit

Many civilizations you are aware of and not aware of, have come and gone. The process of life and humanity has played itself out time and time again. Now is the time for change, once and for all.

The need for change is something that really has manifested in the last 50,000 years of human habitation of some form or another on the Earth plane. As I mentioned before Karma and the Laws of Cause and Effect are playing out. The need to control, the need to possess and take over within the human psyche is something that has developed as part of your physical evolution. This happened to enable you, as a species, to move forward to develop the understanding of physics, science and technology that are provided to enhance your path but not with the understanding of disconnecting of your spiritual nature.

Unfortunately, although many use your energies for common good, they are also those that would use them for negative advancements. This is very much a human thing and not of a spiritual nature. I am not talking about religion, that is another subject altogether.

Your spiritual aspect is who you really are, not the part or role you play in the physical environment. Perhaps this is one of the biggest barriers we need to remove. We can only do that by realizing we are one universe, one spirit and humanity. We are here to share a common journey. We need to heal and unite, not divide and conquer. We need to share and not hoard.

Unconditional love and compassion are the tools we bring into a physical lifetime, but we are conditioned very quickly by government, society and even family to disconnect from this aspect of ourselves. We need to reconnect to move forward into a more meaningful and purposefully existence.

Ideally Equality for All

If you have the technology and an economy that is based on globalization and sharing, then it becomes an ideal opportunity, for equality for all. We could all flourish and grow strong in the knowing we are helping each other.

The existence of life is fragile and needs to be nourished. All the religions have tried to teach us basic truths of universal understanding, they tell us not to learn from our experiences. Love and Compassion is what should nurture us, not violence and war.

Wealth in the physical sense is held in global terms by a handful of people, when compared to the six billion or so souls that are living out their lives on Earth. In many countries governments control the options that individual citizens should have. People are imprisoned for expressing simple truths and beliefs.

Financial greed controls the Earth's natural resources, which are often not used for the common good. The lungs of the Earth, the great forests are being destroyed because the needs of ordinary people are not being met. The oceans are being polluted by human waste, by resources you are not using properly.

Billions and billions are spent on manifesting destruction rather than growth. It was never intended for the Earth to be used for these purposes.

The original intention was and is for good. You need to open your hearts to this universal memory you carry within. You are not owned by anything other than yourselves, you are part of an incredible universe. You have reason to be and to exist on this planet, this jewel within the universe, but remember you don't have unconditional rights to abuse it.

The United Nations was setup for the purpose of equality for all, why does it feel it is falling apart?

We talked about the United Nations; if we were to live by the pretext of the United Nations law and rules and have them working on that level of equality for all human beings then the nature of us, as a species, would change.

So part of the need for globalization, part of the change of that energy, is waking up to that Fifth Dimensional reality. Is to let go of the chains that hold us back, whether we give them to ourselves or we get them from a belief system, or from a political standpoint. There has to be something that is created which we all understand. We all need to be a part of it. We all want to leave a better world for our children to inherit and explore.

I repeat it again and again, but this is a wonderful opportunity to balance your karma, the law of cause and effect. If you leave a world that is destroying itself because of your actions as a species, that is what your children take on. If you leave them a world full of love, compassion, growth and strength, that is what they inherit. The choice would seem easy and yet for many it is hard.

The Great Global Exercise

The division between those that have and those that have not, is something that needs to be more balanced.

It has become a global exercise that needs to be acted on. You are all spiritual beings sharing a common humanity. I have mentioned that technology can be used for common good, and it is wonderful that communication between people is being shared on a better global level. This eventually is, and will, lead to change on a world scale of understanding. In some countries, governments are trying to restrict this global process. The human spirit is strong, eventually it will overcome this control, but it will take time.

Perhaps we need also to talk about patience. Violence and war are not the tools for this change. Knowledge and understanding of your rightful place is perhaps something that could be put to better use with love and compassion.

Peoples in the Developing World countries, as you call them are starting to have access to this technology; they can see what is happening in the rest of the world. This is what will eventually bring down those walls of resistance to change. This brings in a degree of need and want for change. People are realizing there is a big divide and they want the same as everyone else. They want equality and political freedom to determine their own lives.

That doesn't mean you have to take everything away and start from nothing, it doesn't have to be that way. It should be more of an understanding we are all entitled to our birthright. Coming into this world should not always have to manifest in suffering. We can make the choice not to do that, by changing the world we live in, making it a better place to play out our physical experiences. Everyone that lives in your world needs to know this. You control the outcome of what you are playing out.

Chapter Three

What can we do when we don't have the money or the power? How can we be a positive force in all this?

Opening your heart is the first place to start. To connect to the spirit within is the first step to change. This should be followed by the opening of the mind and the understanding of non-attachment to outcome.

Life in your world is very much about the journey. It is not what happens or where you find yourself, rather than what you do with it. If you are given a weapon it does not mean you have to fire it, you do have choice. There are two things that matter in this universe, love and fear. What are you going to let win?

Now there will always be those are in many senses are poor not just financially, but emotionally or are fearful of opening up to love. For there will be some that will choose that type of lifestyle or environment for whatever is needed for the spirit to express itself for the experience. Within that understanding it doesn't mean that someone has to stay in that place for a complete lifetime.

Again everything that we address comes back to reaching out to find our potential. To have the chance to turn adversity into opportunity is what we experience here in a limited environment that is naturally limited by the nature of the frequency rather than the human barriers of control and power.

Within your teachings, within your understanding, perhaps it will be useful to make some expression of this for the generations to come. As I say this is not something that will happen over night, but if you can help one person change or awaken you are making a difference.

This change allows karma that is positive to work for you to help you and others reach their potential. This is why as I mentioned this morning we are trying to work both with individuals, groups and countries where there is the need for change.

Anything in your world that manifests the intention of peace and love is good. We have tried in many different ways, in many time frames, throughout history to bring this message to all.

Follow the God within, to bring an understanding of the journey you are on. It is your right to be able to make that journey without something or someone else controlling it. So it isn't limited by dogma, creed, race, politics, greed, money, for these are not issues that are not attached to the truth of spiritual reality. If you work together as humanity there is more than enough for all, you will not go without, but you will learn so much more about who and what you are.

Coming back to reaching our Potential

Again, everything that we come back to addresses humanity's potential. To give the chance for your spiritual potential to grow and become all that it can be. Within your teachings, within your understanding, perhaps it will be useful to make some expression of this for the generations to come. As I say, we cannot expect people to turn around over night.

If you can help one person change or awaken to the reality of change, then you are making a difference. Learn to "walk your talk". Stay true to the path of your original nature. That is what the great teachers have been passing on to us, this simple truth. This is why as I mentioned this morning we are trying within groups and countries where there is the need for secular lifestyle.

I am not saying that either a spiritual lifestyle or a religious lifestyle is necessary for bringing in that change. It is perhaps better put as a change of intention to the highest good of humanity. We have tried many different things in many different lifetimes.

It is the understanding of the journey that brings liberation and joy that pertains to the ending, so enjoy the moment and live it to your fullest. Don't limit the footsteps you make by dogma, creed, politics, greed, or money. Learn to be content that there is plenty for all.

If you should choose religion or government as your platform, then be compassionate and caring, don't talk of vengeance and hell, control and power for these are of human terms and the darker densities only. REMEMBER GOD, THE UNIVERSE IS UNCONDITIONAL LOVE AND COMPASSION and that you are a manifestation of the universe. Have you not been taught that you have been created in the image of God? To create positive change, just work from your "God Aspect" of knowing. .

The Internet is a phenomenal communication device that can remove those barriers.

JP: That is correct.

Karen: To hear from my friends, that were in the Asian disaster, that day in Thailand, in only moments from the event occurring, was extraordinary. That is how all beings communicate in 5th Dimensional Energy. It becomes tangible.

JP: That's right there is tangibility in that third dimensional world. Again when we wake up to our true nature, our 5th

dimensional energy, we will be able to do it on a personal level if you choose to, but I am not saying that we cannot learn from this expression of energy as long as it is not used to create harm, which on some cases it is. But that again comes back to control and power.

Reveal yourself and trust that god lives within you and every breath you take, for you are god and god is you and you are one. Your mind and the godheads mind are one. The understanding that you share is profound and like a beacon transforms others on their journey to opening their hearts to the truth. For the truth spoken in any form or language is "the truth" for its frequency is truth.

I feel the Earth's energies of healing. Acknowledge the vibration of the Earth's movement and with the breath release the energy. For remember we are all energy and light, we can release and move the trapped energy within, therefore, the pain can go as well.

Give yourself permission to experience this reality as I have previously mentioned. A great majority of us on this planet have been disempowered to believe we cannot heal or shift the pain we endure ourselves. That is a thought that has held us in limitation.

I had a learning experience where Revenue Canada had audited me over a two year period. Talk about an exercise of fear connected to authoritative figures, around superiority and governments. It was a lesson in watching me give away my power habitually without question. I also became aware of the old paradigms we, as humanity had created.

I know I had served many lifetimes where I had been either burned at the stake or put in prison and tortured. That is the physical journey for we are here to experience and be all things. For me, I was choosing to place my energy .and intentions only for the greatest universal good of anchoring love and compassion for humanity and the planet is what I decreed. I made a conscious choice to hold the light so others may wakeup to that choice as well.

I learned I needed to hire an accountant so my energy would be freed up to help others more effectively also the old paradigms needed to be transformed and that people had been disempowered as to what their rights were. I started studying the Magna Charta and discovered a lot. It is in place to protect the rights of the common man versus the government.

I worked with those environmental energies and it wasn't easy. I had physical heart palpitations when I worked through this journey. Now I can receive a letter from them and say," Oh, a letter from my friends and not feel raped or abused by the relationship". I needed to release and heal the negative projections and the wounded perceptions I was holding onto not only for myself, but my compassion went out to humanity. What had we created!

On a sunny day, hold your palm to the nurturing sun and invite it in to every cell of your being. Say yes to it. Then hold it close to your heart as you breathe in its love and support for your journey. Breathe in the sun. With gratitude bless it for it fills your world with love and it is the true mother nurturing and creating life.

Chapter Four

Star Wars

Our feelings are very great and purposeful around the issues pertaining to military decisions that are made on your Earth. There is talk too about using space technology as a form of control and a form of military stance apparently to ward off any other country from firing missiles at other countries within your global arena. Again the law of cause and effect is something to take into account.

With interest I see that some governments are for this and some against it. Unknown sums too large to calculate at any one time are spent on defense and offence. Violence and war are never the right answer. Violence manifests more violence leading to war. Common sense, compassion and love disappear. Power ultimately corrupts.

In times such as these those that pertain to these conditions the perpetrators forget the value of all life. No care is given to the land and the Earth. The destruction of all things is possible which is the highest price, the loss of life.

The gift of the human experience is rare within the universe. The preciousness of this gift is lost in war. Spiritual values are disassociated from, emotions are wrecked and life is damaged or lost, not just for those that fight, but also for millions of innocent victims that are caught and swept up in the destruction. Whilst so much is spent on defense on a global level. Common sense does not reign. Remember that we are all spiritual beings, we all come from the universe, and we are all the same. We all need to be loved and cared for. Those in power need understanding and knowledge of this universal reality.

My concerns however, are not just with the energy on the Earth, but around it too. Universal laws also apply when we are dealing with cosmic energy outside of the Earth's atmosphere and into space. Cosmic energy is still third dimensional; it is not spiritual as such. Although when you look into the night sky you feel your spirit soar because it reminds you of vastness.

Our concern from this frequency is that there are governments and peoples that are planning to send different energy frequencies into the cosmos to further your knowledge of how the universe is built. I am not saying there is anything wrong with reaching for a higher understanding, because that is the reality of your species.

Planning has to be made carefully though because you are still dealing with a physical reality that pertains to the law of cause and effect. Although space around you would appear vast and empty, that is not the reality from this dimension. Life exists within the cosmos in different dimensions. So there is responsibility involved in your process here.

Also of some concern is given by us to those on your planet that would not only try to alter the frequencies within the global atmosphere on the planet, but also wish to experiment into the realms of space warfare as a deterrent.

Please know that enough harm has been done to the web of energy the natural grid systems that surround your planet, just by the infrastructures that are in place. Many billions of your dollars etc. are to be spent on this form of defense, and yet more than two thirds of your planet is under duress and many billions of sentient beings also are living in poverty.

I tell you a universal truth, as we understand it. Space technology will never take off in the way that it is hoped until the problems on your planet are put in order. Yes, you will be able to play out some things but not to your fullest potential.

External to that process, it is with some interest as I watch this process unfold because my main level of understanding and attainment is to help protect the Earth on its own karmic journey. If the energies around the field of the Earth are interfered with, that can and will cause a form of distortion within the energy of your own galaxy and within the universe.

Everything is very finely tuned to keep balance and frequency in harmony with the purpose of sustaining and supporting not only your planet, but many other things too. The consequences of that are beyond comprehension at this stage of the average human mind, because you are not cosmically developed. So you are planning to send a destructive element out in your cosmic system that you have no real understanding of. This could cause harm to other dimensional energies that exist outside of your knowledge.

The Earth and the Cosmos are sentient in their nature and are living entities that are outside of your scientific knowledge at this stage. The laws of cause and effect will still come into play. If you destroy something beyond your comprehension, you will still be help in universal responsibility and that energy will have to be balanced.

Universal process of creation

When the universe was originally created, as you understand it in the third dimension it is not a process that happened within 7 days. It is a process that happened over in human terms a long period of time. But in universal terms it could be a handful of days for time is only linear not multi dimensional. Thought was put into motion the creation of life had to be a processed within the thought and then the thought had to manifest itself to create the structure of the physical universe different to the spiritual universe.

The mind of the godhead of the universe brought in on itself and manifested itself into being in the physical sense to give the reality of space and time so that you could play out in a limited environment. As the cause of this, many other planets, solar system, many cosmic systems within your universe exist and life forms some human or some not. It is still an environment where energies in the third dimension can play out.

As a universal process we have a responsibility of safe guarding that energy for if it is destroyed it will just come in of itself again and again and again. It will manifest itself in greater density. We cannot allow that to happen. We cannot have somebody with a limited understanding interfere with the universal process of creation.

Are you confirming we are not alone in the universe?

Within that understanding, as they say, we need a global recognition that we are not alone in the physical universe. We need an understanding that life exists in different forms, globally on this planet, as well, within the cosmos as you know it.

We as humanity need more respect for all living things, man's ego can be self centered so easily.

There has to be a reverence for life. There has to be an understanding that the world is itself is special and is a living entity. As I say, that is why I am engrossed so very much upon this process of universal karma and Earth karma. We need peace, before you explore the distant stars, which as a species you can do at some time. You have to have an understanding of respect for the cosmos.

No purpose will ever be solved by sending negative frequencies outside the atmosphere. It can only cause chaos. Enough chaos is already held within the Earth's atmosphere, let alone beyond the stars.

So part of the understanding is to help others reach out to put things right here before they start to interfere with anything else. So the form of verbalization is to bring peace, and to bring an understanding of humanity, and then to think about it in time as you progress. When the thought of control and war no longer dominates the force of intelligence behind exploration, you can move forward in compassion and understanding and in growth. Then that is the time to start moving into different understandings and to different ways of dealing with the universe and different cosmic energy, but certainly not for a defense system.

As my heart fills with the vibrancy of the electric alive pink January sunrise the insight comes to me that this rainbow of color unfolds continually around the mother Earth planet. The energy of re birth and the joy filled celebration of the rainbow, liken it to a blanket of vibration, which makes its way somewhere on the Earth. That thought brings great joy and peace to me. I am seeing it all happen at a distance from the place of my original nature.

As you breathe in, and know you are breathing in, then breathe out and know you are breathing out, as Thich Nat Hanh often refers that, in Buddhism, it brings you into the present moment which is made up of the past and holds the unfolding of the future. So being in this present moment is where Heaven on Earth lives and where life is. Nurturing the seeds of happiness and ceasing the nurturing of the not so happy seeds will bring forth an awakened mind which is an aware mind. Mindfulness is the blood to go deeper into knowing. Being peaceful and calm allows the moon or sun of truth to reflect, so the truth can be revealed.

I keep hearing from my guides to be in the moment, just be in the moment and all will unfold. It is trust in the beauty of the universe that will be within. Opening the heart so it can see and experience the truth will hold the energy for others to do so as well, compassionate medicine. Therefore we are in a place of listening with our hearts and open minds so that the insight of the unfolding rainbow may bless you.

Open your heart to come into communion with the energy you are embracing. Breathe into the moment knowing you are breathing in with them in harmony. Breathing out, knowing you are breathing out in harmony, feeling the energies merge and dance in celebration.

The few with power, I can't help feeling in my heart they are not doing God's will.

I have mentioned that this is a time of change. I am not pointing my finger at any one government although there are mass governments in your world that join this conspiracy to undermine life itself. Part of globalization is to open the collective consciousness.

Why should one man, out of billions of people, have the power to destroy because of his understanding? He has no right to do that just as he has no right to destroy any other human being. The concept is they are doing God's will. They are creating their own identity believing they are god themselves. They will try to tamper and play with things beyond their understanding and this need is driven by control and power from others that are around them too.

What are your thoughts on science?

Science and mathematics are the building blocks of the universe, especially in relation to the physical dimension. You could not exist without these building blocks. It is your right to explore and use the physics around you to learn more of your environment. Just use it wisely and it will give you endless useful information. Misuse it and your understanding will not be clear. In universal terms science exists. It is not something that is invented by you, for all things already exist, before they come into Earthy form.

What guidance can you give us for the future generations?

Teach your children to remember their original nature, to love and have compassion. They have the right to stand tall in their world and speak the truth from a universal aspect as they know it. It is only by doing that that you can stop these mad men from taking control of things of which they don't understand. They will help bring globalization into a new standing: we are all equal and need to reach our potential.

Karen: In my practice as a therapist, very often clients second guess their intuition because western medical science doubts the client's inner voice. This doubt is a density in thought which creates insecurity within that individual blocking the truth, that faith can heal or the power of prayer can heal. It seems we have been programmed to need to have physical proof appeasing the mind, instead of bringing in the light, with the intention of healing ourselves. We need to believe we have the capacity to heal ourselves.

JP: There needs to be a balance, as in all things. Science can be an incredible tool, but if wrongly used, it brings confusion. Science is there to produce and awaken and to use in harmony with the physical experience. For many good things come from your learning in science but also as in all things those of a denser mentality will use it to promote denser realities.

It is learning to use it for one purpose and not to misuse it for another purpose that is the essence of this. But as you say, science should grow as you evolve. As you become more aware of your place in the universe, and know what is available to you.

It is to break that cycle of evolvement, to break that cycle into a new understanding of waking up to our potential, using science as a tool to help in this understanding.

Chapter Five

Science has disempowered a lot of people.

JP: 98% of your world is disempowered, but mostly through greed and fear. Help others to see that more clearly, so they can move into empowerment.

Karen: Yes. Thank you, I think it is important to hear that. When people feel re-empowered or empowered to their full potential, the light shines within them. There is this amazing growth and discovery. It is beautiful. I know it is a new beginning for them.

Ignorance can be a form of control.

JP: That is correct. That is why I go back to the start of my talk on globalization in this sense.

If we come from that place where we are all equal, and honor each others humanity then there is no need for ignorance. It can not always be an excuse to stand still. The true nature of our being is move forward in our understanding. Education is a wonderful tool. It is wonderful to be able to find answers to questions of life. Understanding where your place is in the Universe helps you teach others. Helping others to chose the truth rather than ignorance. Know the truth of what you learn in your authentic ear. Reach out to harness this understanding. That serves purpose on the journey you are on.

So as you move forward through these changes with each person becoming more global in their understanding, remember the need to reach out: and not be secular, to be spiritual not necessarily religious, by being a part of humanity rather than just being human.

Re claiming our power

Subconsciously, have we inadvertently given our power away? Has someone taken it? Why are we feeling unworthy, self doubting, small, empty?

From my experiences I have found sometimes that I have freely given away my power, because of my nature or fear. Being in an abusive relationship either at work or personal, the denser energies of control and manipulation can stifle our spirit. For our spirit needs freedom to be in its full expression. We have come into this third dimensional reality as spirit with a physical limitation we do not need any other limitation placed on us as in control or power. We will cover more of this concept later.

I had a spiritual teacher I journeyed with for a time, I bless him for that. A time came where it dawned on me that I felt like a lamb and was struggling with the relationship. I lived in a different city so the distance gave me some clarity and space where I could come to the realization that I felt empty. This was not healthy. I was leaving my partner with whom I had a child

If you would like to try this, hold who it is that you are asking for your power back, call in the person's higher self, and call out for all your power to return to you now. My teacher awoke me to that truth and I honor him for that for it took courage to come to that place of decision to leave or let him know verbally that I did not love the situation. I could not be truly who I was without him judging me. I would go to work and feel huge with energy but I knew that when I came home I made myself small and that saddened me. I know now that it was partly my self-judgment that he was reflecting, but I also knew it was part of my journey to move on.

I sat with the guidance of a friend and asked that my power come back to me from my teacher. All that I gave of my power I asked that it be returned to me now. I was still. All of a sudden it felt like a lightening bolt hit me. I was astonished at the response. It made me giggle for the first time in a while. "Oh there I am," I exclaimed. I felt in that instant quite different. Allow yourself to be creative in this exercise. We give our energy away in many ways: to our government, traditional religions, and our car mechanics. Never doubt your inner voice for it will guide you to where your missing energy has gone. It is in responding and trusting the voice within that the deepest growth begins to happen. Have fun.

This is another energy technique for clearing external energies that pull us off our center. These outside energies can affect us emotionally, spiritually or physically.

As you are seated, extend your awareness outside your body's energy field. If you see, or feel, any strings pulling out from you, acknowledge them as other energies pulling you off center, and with love ask that the blue flaming sword of Archangel Michael cleanse and clearly cut these from you. As they are cut offer gratitude, and send loving energy, or ask Michael to send love in the direction of the string or cord. Surround yourself with violet and gold light from the universe. Asking the universe for its love, protection and direction at all times.

With regards to physical manifestation of pain, I have a place at the upper part of my back where it will ache. Sometimes, I actually can see an energetic hook at my neck. I know exactly who it is because this person will not come around to the front and show themselves, but sneak around d the back to get my attention.

I usually try to cut this attachment, if I still experience the physical pain I will connect with this person's higher-self, asking them to call me on the phone if they need to talk. Very often this person within minutes will phone or I will receive a letter or email. If we can open our minds to that reality that *our physical pain is energy we can start to move it with immediate results. It is very empowering when the physical pain goes instantly; it opens up in your mind to new growth and understanding that we are spiritual beings having a physical experience.*

Chapter Six

The Benefits of Meditation

Jay-Paul: I ask you again to open up to that higher frequency that is available within all of you. When we reach into our higher selves we are reaching into that higher frequency. When we meditate we are opening that gate to the higher frequency. When we are at peace within ourselves knowing that we can reach our potential we are at peace within ourselves. When we go to bed at the end of the day when we have done what we can we are peace with ourselves. When we can laugh and have joy at simple things we are at peace. When we reach out to that spiritual understanding to re-fuel our batteries, we can be at peace.

I notice it is such an effort to keep centered or clear in my mind these days.

But all the times that these negative things occur around your world, it drains us. That is why you are often tired, or disassociate with things around you. Many don't want to see what is happening in your world, it is though you are on overdrive. And yet, you can't run away from the need to change. Very often we have to see what is around us so we can know where to move next. It is not as complicated as a game of chess; it need not be. It takes just a one step at a time to change positions.

The Universe's Compassion

Overall though, we must not loose the essence of understanding of the truth that the universe is compassionate and life continues. Even though these things happen around us, we are all given the opportunity, time, and time again, to put it right.

To re-manifest in a different body, with a different perspective, to bring together the human element and the spiritual element, not just to exist as beasts of the Earth, but exist as spirituals beings within that. We are given that opportunity time and time again.

There is always light after the darkness. I don't want to talk about hope and faith because I think they are irrelevant to this process. I would rather say, as always, it is the knowing within that we can move us on. We have the opportunity time, and time again, to come back and put it right.

To open our eyes and see things as they really are. The universe is compassionate with that. The pain that we all feel in the human body we are compassionate for. It is not something that we wish others to experience but we know that they choose the choices that they make so that they can learn more fully the laws of compassion and unconditional love. That it is within that knowing that once they have acquired that skill that universal understanding that they don't have to keep coming back and redoing it but only through choice they make take on another experience.

Think of it as being like the beautiful lotus and the jewel within; think of each life as being a petal of the lotus. The petals have to fall from the plant from time to time, but with them are carried the seeds of hope. Seeds that will replant themselves that will grow to be another lotus, another blossom of beauty. And again the leaves will fall and the petals will fall, life continues in that cycle.

We have to somewhere along the journey experience what it is to be each petal, a little bit differently from the one before and the one after. We need to experience all those things to become one, to become whole and complete. Know that you are greatly loved for the journey you are on because it is difficult.

You have heard me say many times, a lifetime isn't something that you sign up for once off. This is a contract that you make with the universe for many millions of different experiences. So you are honored for that. It is about the growth and potential so you can create in time your own universes of understanding and knowledge, to add to the universal mind itself.

The manifestation of the universes like itself it creates within itself and of itself. There is talk some times that the universe has reached its furthest boundaries in its physical form and is falling in on itself, that is because you have yet invented what you need as a species to see beyond that.

The truth is that the universe will appear to be folding upon itself but at the same time it is stretching in other directions too. It is not only one energy in one part of the universe but it pertains to all the energies. No more then one single atom in your body pertains to your whole being, but it is still part of you.

So from a universal context life is growing not diminishing. You are likening to a universe, and you are looking through your physical eyes at the physical universe of your being, that causes limitations. Look with your spiritual mind of the vastness and eternity. It is hardly difficult to fathom because it is infinite.

Karen: When you were saying opening your heart, to listening and then opening your mind you are referring to that. Opening to that mind that is all expansive, that greatness, that universal...

JP: An unlimited mind. To know what it needs for the purpose of good. That can help the physical manifestation in life to bring comfort and joy; there is nothing wrong in that. It is only when it is used for destruction that it brings pain and dishonor.

So again here a few thoughts for you to ponder on and to add to the book as you feel is appropriate. It might be something that you like to investigate a little more or talk to me again before you type this particular one. I want it to be part of the universal understanding on the differences between the physical universe and the spiritual universe and how we draw from it and how we are responsible for it.

You have referred to cosmic energies as a third dimensional energy.

JP: Everything that you see with your physical eyes within your universe is of third dimensional quality.

Karen: I have heard you say as well to me that some of us hold or anchor the cosmic energy. As I am sitting here I keep hearing, ask about third dimensional cosmic energy. I am not sure in what regard I am asking that question because as I am expanding I feel my connection to other life forms in other places.

JP: That is correct. Yes. Understand that is the evolvement and incarnation of third dimensional energy. It may be more advanced than the one that you are in, it may be different to the physical reality that you know. There are worlds within the third dimension that are greatly advanced as well and many that are limited. The Earth is caught somewhere between.

That does not mean you don't have the ability to reach out to those on those other levels of understanding and again remember that when a spirit enters on a journey into the third dimension it may not always choose to be in the same place, the same planet. They may choose other third dimensional experiences. But it just so happens within the reality of the cosmos that you live in the Earth as it is going through this process of change and we are swept up in the energies of that, the currents of that.

It doesn't mean you can't connect with other experiences in other third dimensional realities. Remember when I talk of you moving into 5th dimensional energy as an energy within so that doesn't mean there are not beings in other third dimensional physical locations within the physical cosmos or universe that are not connected to their 5th dimensional energy and there are.

So it is a waking up to that understanding not all physical environments are human. Different energies, different gases, have thought process, it is not always spontaneous. It just seems that way because you believe you have control of it in your world.

But if you can wake up to that 5th dimensional energy you are more knowing as I say you listen to it, you hear it and act accordingly. For an example, if you take a beautiful flame, that feeds on the oxygen around you. It brings you light and it brings you heat.

Karen: And Beauty.

JP: And Beauty. Look at the sun in your reality, in your cosmos, in your galaxy; it brings life as you know it into being. You could not survive without it. There is nothing wrong with the original quality of the sun that gives you life. There is beauty in that and there is in all things. It still serves purpose in the physical reality to be part of that great experience. For the sun it is like a mother.

Or you could be a flame from the most beautiful gas on a different planet that is bright blue and feels icy to the touch yet it sustains another form of life. You have no understanding of it in this physical reality but the forces of all universes are all in balance. It's just learning to look from within at this and not with just the human eyes.

As Lyn would say when she sees spirit initially before she sees a form she sees a flick of energy, a wave of energy or a flame of energy. That is our original nature it is of that flame or frequency, but it can manifest itself to look human. It can manifest itself to be anything it needs to be for that experience it is having or giving to someone.

So in some sense you have to look not just at the global picture but the universal picture to really make sense of it.

As an exercise, sit with a flowering plant that is not flowering at the time. See it as having flowers know with your heart that the flowers are within this beautiful plant. Send it loving and compassionate energy holding the focus of the flowers. You may notice within a week the flowers will start to come. I have done this several times with violets, my jasmine plant and the wonderful Christmas cactus. If your plant is not healthy spent some time with it and look deeply as to what the cause maybe. It may want to be moved, put in sunlight for the afternoon or watered. They are sentient beings that are cohabitating with you. Honor them for that.

Chapter Seven

Closing Blessing

Jay-Paul: On that note I am going to withdraw, for I feel I have fed you enough information for now.

Karen: Yes. That's beautiful. Thank you. (Laughter)

JP: I want you to relax and enjoy your journey home and go safely for there is work to be done. I wish you a safe journey in that beautiful sunlit world that you live in.

Karen: My love to you.

JP: And to you it is always there, for I am you and you are me and we are all equal and all have the same understanding. We just manifest different aspects of ourselves, such as those petals on the lotus flower, such as the reflections is a diamond. We just become what we are and what we need to be for expression. You felt that, so with that knowing as always, I give my love back to you and ask that the light of the universe always be with you.

When this discussion came to a close I wept. I realized the work and place we are in as humanity. The journey of peace and freedom for all is integral to our moving forward in our evolution. The understanding and respect for all energies at all levels of existence. The remembering or re connection to our original nature is what we need as a species to grow. It is underway but the journey is a full one.

If this book has touched you, recycle and pass it on. With an open heart teach others how to open their heart so they can listen not with the human ear but with their whole being. That they can open their mind to expand and reach their potential in this lifetime.

My blessings are with each and every one of you. May the light of the universe be always with you.

Part Four

Wave of Change
2012

February 22, 2006

With love and compassion, I share a channeled conversation with Jay Paul regarding life as humanity and how we can prepare ourselves, for this wave of change. This talks about our tiredness, pain and the density of third dimensional energies that are frantically trying to undermine this change into pure light and fourth dimensional frequency.

I have been very tried, and with compassion Jay Paul wanted to address this. Many forces are influencing me moving forward at present. One, my daughter and her personality, a new relationship that has old way energy still attached or playing out and the other was the cancer cells and hormones in my physical body that needs attending to.

In between our cells is space. The space in between our cells can hold density or light. The denser energies right now are playing out, coming into our physical bodies. If two cells are surrounded by this energy then it can have an effect on our systems in our physical body. These energies do not want to anchor into solely our physical but the multi dimensionality of who we are. We have the physical, emotional, mental, spiritual, astral bodies, our aura, higher selves and the ripple of all of who we have been through time. This consciousness has purpose or means business. In looking around the planet one can see it at work on many levels.

The urgency to be diligent in keeping these spaces filled with brilliant loving universal light is integral to our surviving this change or shift. Keeping in balance and harmony with regards to our health, is important. I see from my perspective, poor health, as being out of balance.

It is in our intention to be of service to the highest and greatest good of humanity. For man's inhumanity to man must cease, and man's humanity to man, must expand. It is time.

A few years ago, it was documented that solar flares from the sun had left and were moving through space. Science has recorded this and measured it. The energy of those flares is for purpose and are coming towards the earth, in this unique Milky Way galaxy. Its purpose is to infuse all sentient life forms with a higher vibrational frequency altering the third dimensional illusion to fourth dimensional reality. I refer to the third dimension as illusion because the third dimension and the density is an illusion that has been playing out for millennia.

It is important, as we are distracted with this density, which may wear the mask of a friend, nightmares or pain may it be known, as an illusion. The reality of living in a place where thought is instantaneous, where love and compassion exists in all humans' hearts is a reality.

Two incidents occurred around identifying the denser energy playing out in my life; one being my illusion of tiredness, which was stopping me from moving forward; and in a few friends that were allowing this energy within them to have voice. I could see that the density had entered into their thoughts and had thrown them off centre. I could have got attached to the density and started playing out in the drama that could have unfolded, but I didn't. Placing my hands outwards with blessings is transformational for that energy. We do have choice. We can choose to respond with love and compassion or with fear, pride and ego.

Know that nothing can harm you and without a shadow of a doubt, the light is stronger than the density, and will help you. That deep knowing is a freedom from illusion. It will bring you peace.

Protection, Protection, Protection, This does not come from fear as some may surmise, but out of necessity as this shift draws near. I personally, can feel this change as a reality and my heart is joy filled with the blessing that is to come upon all sentient beings.

In many ancient times previous to this, the shifts have come but not with the results that are pre determined here. Many suffered in the wake of Atlantis and Lemuria and are here now to help support this change. Fear is rampant and to know in your hearts that the energies that be, are surrounding the planet Earth with their etheric hands holding it steady when the time comes, should liberate your fear.

The energy that is coming through this galaxy will travel through, not hit the earth planet, but travel through the spaces between the cells of all sentient life forms. The spaces of light will receive a boost of this energy which will instantly transform us into the fourth dimensional energy. Our original nature or spirit will be merged in unity with the physical. It has been said as third dimensional beings we have 80% of our spirit in our bodies and the other 20% remains in spirit where we are connected by a silver cord.

Thought will be instantaneous. We will be able to manifest a building we need to live in or for our work. There will be still the need for retreat, learning, and meditation. The teachers will be teaching the new way for those that are suffering the loss of family members who did not make it through the shift. Those of us holding onto old ways, thoughts, belief systems, in essence the density that surrounds the cells will repel this energy. They will be taken to another illusion where they can continue to play out and balance the denser energy. When they are ready they will join this reality if they so choose.

It will last three days. The sun will rise and as the evening approaches the sun will stay in the western sky for two days, depending on where you live on the globe. The third day it will be dark for 24 hours and then the sun will rise to the dawning of a new day in fourth dimensional reality in the east. The vibrancy of color will change for we will see with our fourth dimensional eyes.

The key is to know in your hearts that you are loved and hold the frequency in the spaces of who you are with firm belief that you are the light of the universe.

February 23, 2006

Support and help each other as light workers for this dense energy will try to undermine your purpose. I and Lyn Inglis came into this lifetime pre-determined to work with the higher frequencies in assisting with the success of this shift. From birth, we have been undermined with sexual, emotional abuse and physical co-habitation that resulted in deformity. Helping each other remain clear and balanced in the light with pure intention of love and compassion is a 24/7 job. It can be draining. I suggested swatting the energy away using a tennis racket and Jay Paul's comment was that the racquet had holes. We had a good laugh.

A few weeks ago, I started working with the image of looking down from my higher self to my physical body and seeing the denser frequencies as webbing that was blocking or affecting an area of my body. I took what looked like butterfly netting and gently scooped away the debris. It was a beautiful feeling in my physical body as the physical pain or ache actually, to my surprise, dissipated. It was then I met the Lama who greeted me with open arms and no protocol but as old friends re-uniting. The light show in my head from that moment was extraordinary.

Many teachers and students will come forward before this wave of change in the last remaining years, to help with clarity and balance. This Tantric Lama here from Tibet, has opened my remembering to a lifetime with him, as a past student. It has been a joyous connection, filled with excitement for me, a beautiful strong energy and light of the universe to embrace and cloak me in these times of density. Lyn and I have become his students.

February 28, 2006

Introduction

At the Medicine Buddha Empowerment Ritual on Monday, February 27, there were some common themes that ran parallel with my afternoon talk with Jay Paul.

The Lama talked about appeasing the spirits that would cause obstacles on our path. For example, a couple from Red Deer cancelled their healing appointment with him because the roads were bad. His interpretation of that was, it was an obstacle. He also shared that tiredness, sleepiness, lack of focus, depression was all work of the spirits, undermining our journey of light and creating these responses in us to stop us from moving forward.

I sat with an "Aha moment", remembering what Jay Paul had said with regards to illusion or delusion and how it plays out in our lives. In this ritual, a formula was created by the Lama, powerful and attractive to the spirits. He shared that the magnificence of the barley flour he used with butter was all that they aspired to. As they lit it, and said prayers, they placed it at the back of the room with the understanding that they would be attracted to it and therefore create the space for us to be open to the energies of the white light of the healing Medicine Buddha. The image that came to mind was similar to placing a dish of beer out on a saucer when one is at a picnic gathering, so the flies leave the picnickers alone. Of course, it was much more profound than that.

With love, I transcribe the afternoon conversation with Jay Paul to serve as a light amongst the distractions or the obstacles, which we allow in our lives. With purpose and urgency, I hold the understanding that we can consciously be aware of the obstacles that are created and choose to act with love and compassion in our hearts, rather than out of fear or anger, for we do have choice. As we choose with love and compassion, we do so for all sentient beings. As we commit to healing ourselves, we do so for all sentient beings.

My voice will appear in italics.

With Love I give you, Jay Paul

You are tired at the moment, and I want to talk to you about that. You have been out of balance, Karen, and we don't want you to be drained. I just want you to be able to settle into your energy, in your own space, rather than being manipulated or feel that someone is taking more energy from you than you are able to give. It seems unfair. I know the best of intentions are there, but we do have choice. When we choose to contract, we are making ourselves denser and with that choice like a ripple effect, it affects other events in ones life. A person is choosing to draw themselves down where they can be lifting themselves up, this is sad to see.

Karen: Personally, this is happening for me in my family life. A family member is choosing this and it is draining.

It is important to be honest with them in your heart and throat centre. If you feel that they are sucking you dry, then say so. You need to let them see that side of you, "I need your support, rather than you working against me." Be in your truth. Do it with love.

I am aware of your energy field being stretched at the moment. I am aware of people around you that draw on you, physical things and other energies around you as well. We try to put a blue and green energy crystal around you to protect you but everything is being undermined at the moment. It is the intention of density.

This is the time now where we are getting to a place, where this is the darkest hour before the dawn. These energies know they haven't got long to play out, so they are attacking in any way, shape or form that they can. Even in some of the people that you are connecting with. You are being imploded with other people that are picking up on this energy and are not thinking about it, not expressing it appropriately, and just throwing it at you. It is the denser frequencies that are working with them, trying to undermine in little ways, in very subtle ways. It all adds up.

One of the things I want to talk to you about, is balancing your energy around you on an emotional level. I honor you and your relationship with Willy, but it is still coming together. It hasn't reached its potential yet. Sometimes, you get a glimpse of it and it is gone. Some of these energies are playing out around Willy. It is causing stress for you, so it brings in that tiredness, that lack of motivation to move forward.

These are all barriers that are presenting themselves to see your response. Know them for what they are, because they are an illusion, in the truest sense of the word. If we connect with them as they are, and know them as a reality, then they will play out. If you connect with them as an illusion, they will let go. If you are attached to a response, then you play out in the drama. I know you try really hard not to get brought in, but sometimes other people are acting out in the drama and you have no control over that. It can be draining witnessing it or being in the energy, of those that do that.

This is quite a dense time for you. On top of that, your energy levels are low at the moment, as I have said. I know you are seeking help with why this is so. From the perspective where we come from, I just want to point you in some different direction for consideration. There are certain tests that people want to do to manipulate your physical systems which really won't play out in any form. So be cautious with what is given or suggested to you even though they are given with the best intention. I am concerned with your level of energy, partly to do with the thyroid, so doing the saliva test is a good idea. The hormones need re balancing.

So I am saying it is these darker energies, trying to squeeze in, in any way that they can.

I talked to you before about the theory or hypothesis which is coming into understanding about the space around all the cells. It is happening at the moment, because of the nature of the environment of the earth and the density that is playing out. You have to make a total commitment to the understanding that you fill those spaces up, with every sequence of work that you do, only with light of the highest understanding that you know.

What is happening is some of the density is trying to sneak into those spaces and you are strong enough that it won't take over, but you have to have the intention that you will not let any in, at all. The nature of these energies is that they will sneak into a few cells and it will change the whole system, as to how you are built and how you respond. You have to remember, that in the reality that is opening, that the blossom of the flower that is opening is a different reality to what you have understood in the past. You are not just linear and physical; you are multi dimensional as we have said before. You get the understanding of the multi layered chess board if you like.

I will take a moment to explain what Jay Paul means in this analogy. If we can imagine many hundreds of chessboards stacked on top of each other and they spiral, always moving. Let's say that sometimes the places of squares line up to another incarnation that you have had. You may have an experience of that in your awakening state. For instance, when I went to Maui I knew as I lay on the beach I felt myself

160

lying on the beach in Lemuria as well. My awareness had a multi dimensional experience. We have been all things.

You are so much more than your physical aspect. You are those spaces between those cells and they manifest in that way of being multidimensional, so the different energies in different arenas, can play out in that understanding. When the energy flows in that way, it can attack those physical spaces, with the understanding in that, that you are not just your physical body, mind and emotional structures they are still related to the physical but can lead to the spiritual. You have your aura, your astral body, your spirit, your higher self or ethereal self. So you are not just your physical being, you are a multi dimensional being.

What is happening is that these darker energies are trying to get their way, not just into the physical but the multidimensional part of you. Trying to weave their way in, they can try to undermine the other aspects of yourself and you can loose your connection to your spirituality.

They know that the multi dimensional frequencies, the fourth and fifth dimensional energies, are going to win this battle. It is not a matter of if, rather of when, and sooner, rather than later. The density is trying to break into more than just the physical, so you are tired on many levels of your being. It is not just a physical, mental or emotional tiredness, it is on many levels.

You talked of, a space inside yourself which is created, that the dense energy is trying to get into. If it gets into that space and creates darkness, you can understand the spiritual disassociation. Now is the time to fill that space with light in the truest understanding that you know. This is the time for the warrior energy to come into for protection.

These energies are trying to bring that same type of mentality into being, again referring to the Auschwitz energy. In treatment, when someone is releasing this energy and you feel pain or distraction, they are moving the energy enough around you to give you the memory of it. It is only an illusion, for that energy will never be again.

That reality has been and never will be again for you in this lifetime, but that doesn't mean it won't try to move in and pertain to the illusion, or the delusion, if your want to call it that. It is your mind knowing beyond any doubt, that what you have in place for protection and support is the truth. Everything else that is around, like the doubt that comes in your mind is irrelevant. Its journey is to undermine and slip into those spaces that are vacant. Its purpose is to undermine in a very slow and meaningful way.

Trust the knowing of whom you are and that your journey is supported. You know beyond doubt, that you are stronger than the illusion, because you are the reality. You are the multi dimensional and physical reality of your spiritual nature. You are. I am. We are. That is the truth of the original nature.

The energy of illusion is shadow energy. It attacks in the shadows. It tries to undermine the purest of thoughts in the shadows. For an example, you are aware of nightmares. It can not get in physically while you are consciously awake or when I am with you. It will try and sneak into the sub conscious mind when you are detached from your body. It tries to play out and undermine the intake of energy in that way. That is why others are having nightmares as well. It is trying to get in, in any way that it can. It is an illusion. That is why the dreams seem absurd. They are just trying to play out, in the only way they know how.

See yourself like the mountains here, strong, solid as a rock, and know that anything that is sent to you, that is not acceptable to you, is an illusion.

I want to honor the projects that you are continuing for me and that I honor you, for you are trying to get the word out to the world, as you understand. To break the illusions, to open yourself to higher consciousness and understanding, for that is the way of the future.

These energies have been manifesting for over thousands and thousands of years, they have only a handful of years to play out. The energies around are just wanting to stop the process. They are limited. They are only third dimensional energies.

The universe that you know, that you live in, is part of the galaxy, is part of the cosmos, and is part of the great sun, the original Rah, which gave life to the cosmos within the universe. It is the same energy that is changing. You are at a stage now, if you think of your planet at the edge of the Milky Way and this vast galaxy is bigger than anything you can imagine; it is just a small part of the universe. The center of this galaxy is an incredible cosmos or Rah energy that is special to your Milky Way galaxy. It is unique.

This energy from the original Rah, the original God, however you want to put it, is traveling at the speed of light to your universe. It is traveling in its own pattern changing the frequency of things as it comes upon them. This energy has now traveled so far that it has even come to a place where it is in your galaxy. in your cosmos, in your solar system. It is playing out with the understanding that your sun is losing the polarity as we know it, the sun is still strong and still there.

There have been solar flares in the last few years that have changed weather patterns and peoples behavior, it has now left the sun and has done what it needed to do there, and it is moving nearer the earth. Within a handful of years, in earth time as you know it, it will filter through the earth too.

That will lead to a change in the energy. First of all, the magnetic poles will be affected. This has already started to happen and you know that. It has changed already a few degrees with some of the earth's natural changes, like the tsunami. Karma is playing out on the planet. What was north will be south, what was east will be west. It will turn around completely the axis of the planet. Doing that, it will realign the planet in such a way it will be able to absorb this fourth dimensional energy. Then, it will return to a pattern where it can carry on existing and playing out.

This energy is renewing the earth. This energy is renewing every sentient life form. This energy is even renewing our understanding of spirit, too. So again it is the pebble affect in a far bigger motion as we talked of before.

We need people to understand what this change is a result of. This change is a blessing for the planet to give it rest and to help it to heal.

What is going to happen in this time is that there will be many that choose to exit the earth. It is already starting to happen, through weather systems or because they have pre determined understanding, which will be played out. Those that are left behind will be able to survive and carry on picking up the pieces, so to speak. They have an understanding of the thought process of the higher self. In other words, they are awake to fourth dimensional energy.

There are children that are coming into this world that already have the understanding. Those will be the future. For you that are the older ones, if I may call you that, which is left behind here, will make the footprints in the sand for the children to follow, you are their teachers.

For those that exit the earth, there will be much sadness. Understand that their energy will be taken and be given opportunity after opportunity to incarnate in another third dimensional reality that will honor them as they are and what they know. They may play out their own expansion of energy until they are ready to incarnate into fourth dimensional energy again. They may not come back to the planet earth to continue their journey or they may choose to. It is irrelevant, but I want you to know we need to bring an understanding to the people of the earth, of the change that is happening, of the need to connect more fully with love, compassion and understanding for the earth and all sentient life. To understand that there is a great power of love that shields this world that wants it to move gently into this new understanding.

There are many of us, including myself, that are involved in the karma of the earth and the cycle of life, that hold this energy, dear. We hold our arms around the earth to protect it and all that we can.

The purpose of this exercise is not to bring fear. It is to bring love into the place where it needs to be. When you grow in love, you grow in intention of being part of the universe. The earth is ready for change and it can't wait any longer.

We are talking about many changes still to happen. There will be occasion where fear will be in many hearts. There will be occasion where those will rear up and say," God has deemed this and this is punishment". Understand that is not the truth. The universe has deemed this, to allow for you to awaken to a new dawn, to a new conscience and honor the earth, as you know it. There will be those that follow you and come after you that have this same understanding.

There will be those that are in fear that walk in judgment. Over come the obstacles with love. Do not fall into fear. For again, I know that it is touching the hearts of a lot of you light workers from time to time. It is natural for you have been here many times before. It is natural that you have experienced when the darkness has won over the light.

Atlantis and Lemuria went in that way, though it hurts my heart to say that. If you know that life changes from one instant to another and energy is never wasted, the tragedy is less, if you understand this.

We can not bring this fourth dimensional energy into a world where there is the have and the have-nots. When there are those that have a universal understanding and those who would put the illusion of fear in people's faces.

It is out of balance right now. There are those that would die for their belief systems and their belief system will take them to where they understand. It is an illusion too, for at some stage they have to see the reality of their choices.

You have the understanding when you left the earth in those times of change, even though the earth continued in third dimension energy within you leaving, you would have gone to a place of higher dimension or higher frequency, the spirit world. Know that you have tasted that fourth dimensional energy in a different way, in a different place. That is the place between lifetimes that is the place you go for learning, for giving and receiving. Learning how the creation of all things manifests. You can't do that in third dimensional energy.

You have talked recently about the need to be in that space, the need to feel that higher frequency, the need to go home. There has been an aching in your heart and in others of the need for something different, a place where you can go where there is safety and peace, where there is knowledge, not ignorance. Where there is love and not fear; where there is potential; not limitation. You are wanting this now because you are recognizing the density of energies that are around you, are trying to stop the change and you are so close.

When you pass from the third dimensional energy you make that leap of faith, into that higher frequency, rather than having to transmute your energy from the physical to the multi dimensional. This energy coming into the earth will make it possible to exist in the earth in that energy and with the axis change, time as you know it from a third dimensional world, will exist to be a limitation.

In this fourth dimensional world that is coming into being, you are fighting, with all that you know. You are fighting for that place where you know you are meant to see that new day dawn and you are meant to live in the physical world without limitation of time. You may wonder why you are not young in experiencing this. In this new frequency, time will cease to exist as you know it. Age will be irrelevant. You will be young in this understanding. Death will be a process that occurs through choice rather than dying of a physical to force you into another frequency. As all choice leads to different adventures, you will need to experience fifth dimensional energy as well. So from time to time the choice will be made to exit. It will be a choice not a necessity.

Things will change in a very different way. Losing the concept of time, one of the advantages of multi dimensional energy again does not know time or distance. The way of manifesting your thought process will be those of what you know in spirit, it will be instantaneous. You will be able to manifest in your lives, the buildings you need to live in, the environment you wish to be in, the people you want around you, the guidance you wish for and the teachings you wish to give. Those that come into your understanding, you will have choice as to how that manifests. Reality will be very quick. The reality is instantaneous. It will be a very different understanding from what you know.

This comes from that energy that is moving towards you. It will not alter on a cellular level but make the response to cellular change very different. The reaction will be different rather than the physical. We have talked about every space and filling it with light, we have talked about the space between every particle that exists. Right now, the darkness can come into any of those spaces if it is allowed or that you can over ride that and let love and compassion into the spaces to bring light.

When the energy comes for those that hold light in those spaces, the fourth dimensional energy will enter and fill those spaces because it is attracted to the light. Those that are stuck in density, it will repel. That is the change in the life that will continue. This energy will literally bombard the earth and travel through it.

Those that are open to receive, that can understand the practice of love and compassion can step aside from the ego and the drive that causes destruction. They will receive that light and it will change them forever. For as I say, this is the space that needs to be filled and it will make the cellular reaction to things different. The component of each structure will change as a result of this energy coming in. It won't just come in and leave; it will come in and stay.

Those that are repelled by the light and are restricted in their understanding, it will force them to travel their pre determined path of leaving the earth and be in an environment that can still sustain them, so that they can still play out the illusions of what they need.

We do not wish to create any harm, you understand that. No energy is destroyed because of this. All energy is given the opportunity to move on and learn because of this. When they are ready, the choice of where they incarnate or stay, it remains for them to make.

It is literally, for those that are open, charging your batteries.

Like sand blasting a building if there are irregularities or density it will repel or crumble.

Where that space is open to give and receive love that space will blossom. It will help transform the planet as you know it in a small amount of time because thought will be instantaneous.

As we talk about Shangri-La, the hidden valley, the world will become a Shangri-La. It won't be hidden; it will be the way of things. There will be a place to learn and a place to grow. There will be many experiences to have, that you have known and those that are very different, for it will not sustain density.

The density will not come back. Once every space that is left in a living force on this planet, is left with this energy, it will never return to the darkness, it will not be able to. Although there is some fear and trepidation in the hearts of many about what this change means for you as individuals, as well for you as a species, as well as for sentient life on this planet and things that you know as real around you. The fear will be taken from you and you will see with the eyes of your higher self, you will see from the spiritual, the whole picture rather than part of the picture. You will awaken to an alignment here.

I have mentioned to you and a few others that when you come into this lifetime only a part of your spiritual nature comes in. With this energy coming in, your spiritual self will be in complete alignment with your physical self. It will be not a question of having your spirit here or one part there, it will not be separated, your higher self will be incorporated into the mind and the body, so when you make decisions and learn you are then totally not only open to your higher self, but to the universe. The higher self will be incorporated so that the universe will be closer.

Do not be in fear of the change for the change will be wonderful. The fear is in the anticipation of these dark energies playing out to try and stop.

You will be able to separate the illusion from the reality. Put your hands out and extend it with compassion for those that will go through this in fear for they will have a difficult journey. Ask in your heart for the universe to manifest what they need so that they can play out in a total understanding of the reality as they know it what they need then to be able to then awaken to the full connection of what they are. Man's inhumanity to man has to change, and man's humanity to man has to grow in love and understanding, that we are all the same. As I say, we are, you are, I am.

The reality is as they say in biblical terms; it is to bring the kingdom to heaven, the light into the darkness, nirvana into everyday life. It doesn't matter how you approach it, there is a place, and this change is at hand.

There is fear, much fear in your world. Even though there are those that may not understand this change, they know that something is happening. Perhaps somewhere in their souls they know but can't find the words to express it, so they cling to illusion and fear because it held them steady in the past. "If somebody else is making this happen then I don't have to take responsibility for it and I can stay in fear", are some thought patterns. They don't have to take responsibility.

In Buddhist terms, you can understand that this change will bring nirvana.

Some may choose to leave this higher frequency and work with the others still in the third dimension, for whatever need, needs to be fulfilled, whatever gift of love they are giving. There will be those who move forward to this understanding as well, for there will still be the need for guidance from time to time, the need for practice, peace, meditation and retreat.

We are only touching the tip of the iceberg here.

We need to send out words of wisdom of this change for those who are opening up so that we can open a window of light for those in fear.

Maybe when the new dawn comes we will not have to have the words sent out for all will know, those inner gifts of telepathy or of understanding, I believe you call it "extra sensory perception", really it is to be awake, to your own intuition.

This wave of new energy will bring the dawn of a new day. It will hold a day or more in a length of time during this change and revert back, to a similar pattern. It has happened before in earth's history and has been documented before by the Mayan, the Hopi and Ancient Egyptian. Lemuria knew of it, too.

Our element of self doubt comes from the darkness, whether we are worthy. The darkness came early in your life because of what you pre determined. The darkness came in, and then the light came in. You know deep inside, there is a place for you but your self esteem is low sometimes. Support each other, when fear comes in reassure your partner with love and compassion. Be there for each other.

In this place of awakening, there will not be the need for drugs to alter things, for anything to stop the flow of natural energy and its processes. Disease, depression, cancer will not be able to exist in those higher energies. There is already continents that are covered with disease and virus that is the exit for many before this change. If your disease is a cancer and another's is depression. One is emotional and one is physical but the intention of those energies is to undermine.

Know that when you wake up in that new dawn and move forward into that light of understanding, the need for drugs or anything else will not be part of that understanding.

Karen: We are timing our healing for this new change.

It gets back to the spaces to fill those spaces until this wave of energy comes in.

Try to do that physically and emotionally by breathing in the light and fill in that space; do not let that energy in that space. It is a question of releasing. Remind yourself that you can make choices in love and understanding, instead of fear. In that energy, you can only make the choices out of love and light. That is what your journey is in the next few years.

Already on a daily basis your paths are opening up to new understandings as people get in touch with you. The pupil is there for the teacher, for the pupil chooses the teacher. But the teacher manifests when the pupil is ready also. There is much learning and direction that is playing out for you to help support you, as this time of change gets nearer and nearer, to try and give you what you need to get from this space, to that. So allow those energies to come in and feed you, to heal you and to nourish you, for they come from a higher frequency too and you will not be drawn to that which is ignorant.

Karen: Is the Lama that has come to Canmore and Banff, a teacher or pre determined connection for Lyn and me?

The Lama is an example of that. This will support you and not let the darkness in, to recharge you with that love and compassion and everything that is good. It breaks away the illusion, it breaks away the fear. So you are ready for this wave of energy to touch you, hold you, enfold you and liberate you.

There are many conversations out there around this, as there are ways of expression. It is just getting through this in between time in the third dimension where time exists. You are ready and when you need to manifest something, project it in that way and treat it as if it has already happened. You have to be able to survive and live in this third dimension world. As it fades out, you still have to support yourself physically, emotionally and spiritually. You have to be able to feed yourself in all those ways, so if I can touch base from time to time and help feed the part of you that knows this, to refill you with that knowledge that you hold and bring it to a more real space, where you can work with it, I would be pleased to do that.

It is a difficult time a time of change and uncertainty. This energy will work in any way that they can to stop you from moving forward. Using love and compassion and reaching out to others is like a sharp knife cutting through the density.

I see before you many changes coming, in the next few weeks. You will not always sit in this bed at this window in this way, for there is change for you at another window, another window of opportunity, a place where life will take on a different meaning, a reaching out and sharing, a blending, a coming together. That road will sometimes be easy and sometimes difficult but holdfast to your truth as you know it and it will hold you steady in that change. I wish you well on that journey.

The denser energies hold back creating limitation, not potential. With the bringing together of these two families, you want to make things as easy as possible for your future. For you move as a family, into this new energy. The understanding is to move away from the old ways that hold us back. The understanding too, is to be in this physical reality to find love and to able to appreciate the bounty and the beauty that comes with that. A different way, to how we do in the higher frequency. Your journey is to experience those things, too. You have to be in the understanding and be firm, direct and honest but loving and kind with it too. It is not always what is said but the way that it is said. Angel too, there is a new home, one that she has had a taste of, but slightly different. She will be fine.

Karen: How about my partner?

Part of the understanding of his, is that he knows that there is change and it is easier to hold on to what he knows then see where it takes you. His hold with his family is so deep but it is done with love. He needs to seal the past to move forward into the future, without anything holding him back.

It is the diligence of the practice, for us to move forward without fear.

Karen: I find it amazing how if I need to get this cancer piece out that there has been no one to help me.

Again, it is the darker energy. I would not play games around this.

Karen: I got caught up in the trip up. I started to believe that maybe there is nothing to concern myself about.

I want to tell you Karen, that you have a part to play in this change and nothing will stop you, whether you treat it or not, but it could affect your quality of life from now and then. It is something that needs to be removed or drained off, drain the fluid off that is all that it needs at this stage. What we don't want it to do is get bigger and burst of its own accord. Then it will send that frequency of cancer into your whole body. It is simple

Karen: I will give the doctors that guidance then. I don't have the tools to do it myself.

I don't want you wasting your energy. Remember all those cells have spaces too. Send the light into those spaces. Yes, I would not leave it; we want you strong and well. We don't want you being so tired. I am sure some of those cells are making you tired, as well as other things, we talked of.

I say this with reference for you and Lyn both; you have got to keep yourself in balance. You have avoided this responsibility for some time, for your temples. Encourage each other to be vigilant. You need balance to get through this change.

I am smiling, because it is intention that will free you. Many take supplements and are unwell. Some eat chocolate and coke and they are well. It is perception and the intention that if it won't hurt you, so be it. If you believe something can hurt you it will, if you believe it, it won't.

Karen: If I eat a cookie thinking that it will make me gain 10 pounds, it will.

It is all about the mind and being mindful. Not too many extremes but being in balance and harmony.

Give honor to whatever it is that you put into your temple and you will be fine. It is only ashes to ashes, then dust to dust very quickly, this is the physical reality. With this new energy coming in, the structure of that will change to.

Karen: So when that energy comes in and the cells are vibrating with that joy and celebration, our higher selves merging in totality, will that take a time of integration or will it be as thought is instantaneous?

It will be instantaneous. There maybe a few pauses for thought as the adjustment happens, but only pauses.

Karen: I look forward to it, with bated breath.

When you look out the window you will see as though the sun will stay in the sky in one point in the west, it will not sink below the horizon and the day will extend to make three days. Then there is darkness for a day and a ray of light in the east. You will know then, during the extended day depending where on the globe you are, to not be in fear that you are part of this change. During the rising of the sun, the non setting of that sun this wave of energy will have passed through everything, totally, the whole expanse of your planet through to the very centre of its being, through every mountain and every valley; through every ocean and every trench; and every country and all the land masses.

Then it will carry on once it has left the earth bringing change to the outer areas of the galaxy, then it will implode on itself. It will be as though creation has a new start.

Karen: Magnificent.

Think of it as in terms of color. Velvet violet and indigo smooth and silky, gold energy almost transparent in its existence, blending with that other frequency that is velvety is nature bringing peace and bringing love. It is though the universe is mending itself, awakening to a new conscience. The universal mind as an expression of that new consciousness will touch everything that exists. That is what this wave of energy is about. It will make available the threads of the universe to all who want to use it. It will make available the knowledge of the ancient in the whole time of the planet, a beginning, a reality of history that has been buried. Mankind's coming to the earth, merging to the earth, coming into species, in their own right. Everything will become plain as day, the illusions will be gone.

Lemuria was the original Garden of Eden, and though it is carried in memory, somewhat in Biblical nature, years ago and in miles not so far, mythological in its existence,

Lemuria did exist. Energy changes happened frequently, that is where life started as you know it on the planet.

I am aware of time moving by and I am aware that it is a precious thing for it will not last for long. Even from the understanding that it is only a few years it is nothing at all. It is though I just look and see that reality is so close.

Karen: That is what I feel, it is almost like it is cushioning up against me.

That is correct. Our work, or those that share my understanding of consciousness, are putting our hands around the earth, holding it steady for this change. As I said, I am involved in the evolution of the planet and the karma itself, all is coming to manifest now for purpose.

These messages I tell you are limited on your planet. I do bring through the same message in different places and different cultures, but I want you to know that for this area of the globe, the northern continent, the northern country, the vessel I use is limited to this. That is why it is important that the word get out.

In other areas I manifest in different ways but the message is the same.

Karen: How do you see this text taking form?

I want you to organize events for people to talk about this. Project it with text or word.

Karen: You can count on me.

We would not be working together if I didn't.

When I come to you, I speak and say that I am made up of millions and millions and millions of energy that come together to work in harmony, balance and understanding.

This is where I invite you. The coming together of all things is the next part of your journey.

I am not going to talk much more I feel the energy of Lyn needs to be nourished as you do. I want to thank you again for the opportunity and I thank you for choosing this path in this lifetime because to serve purpose does make a difference, bringing the light of understanding into people's hearts is the greatest gift that you can give them. So I bless you and honor you for your choice, for those that you work with. You are the light of the universe and it will always be with you.

March 24, 2006 Synopsis of March 23rd meeting

Dear Ones

Last night we all had the wonderment and privilege to be in unity at Willy's home to learn more as teachers of the new way, and to understand these waves resulting in the many changes that are currently happening within and around us.

This information and teachings are coming forward to us as humanity, not to breed fear but to shed a universal understanding around all that is occurring at present and that will unfold.

Jay Paul, re iterated how Mother Earth is healing herself and the density that has been breed over millennia has to be transformed into a higher frequency so the new way of being can be experienced on this planet. This new way is a learning curve for spiritual growth as spiritual beings.

The Wave of Change is half way completed. Changes started in 2000 and will continue until 2012. If we as humanity can shift the consciousness with ease and grace then the earth will not need to create an event that will cause change to happen with intensity.

Be at peace in this knowing that the universe loves all sentient beings and holds supporting energy for all of us in this moment.

We can choose to act out of love or fear in this illusion, we play out on Earth.

Please know the density, for it is an illusion. Be in your hearts and with diligence practice love and compassion for yourself. Like the pebble being thrown into the pond, it will ripple out to those around you, your community, and all sentient beings. In saying this, I am reminding you that energy is never wasted.

As Jay Paul can see into the future, his advice is to hold love in your hearts in these times of trouble, as it is the darkest hour before the dawn, spread the word of love so all may experience this change with ease and grace and the joy filled experience of being here on the Earth planet at this time, in service. A key is that deep unshakeable knowing that we are all God.

March 23, 2006 group meeting with Jay Paul on "The Wave of Change"

I am known as Jay Paul I use this name when I work with Lyn and Karen as it is something they can identify with. I come to you in greetings and in light, and wanting to share the benefit of my understanding with you, as a way of learning and reaching into a greater understanding of the changes that are currently happening presently and into the future.

When I speak, I am not asking for forgiveness, just the understanding that it is important in our work we approach it from a serious standpoint, but I believe, in the understanding of the universe, that there is a license to bring humor in when it is appropriate.

I don't want to appear any different from who you are because we are all universal energy; this is what we share in common. I have just chosen to experience to work from this side, just as you have chosen to live and experience the third dimension at this time.

You all have seen some of the words that have been printed and expressed. Let's use some of the time this evening to ask questions around what you have read. If there is something that you don't understand or want me to give further information, I would be happy to do so.

Karen, I just want to take this opportunity to thank you for the time you have given freely, so that these words could be manifested and printed and sent out into the world.

Thank you to you as well Lee, for your expertise in design and bringing things together.

For you too, Janet, for some of the editing that you have given on this, I understand that this is the process and wish to thank you.

For all of you, those have been kind enough to read these words and try to bring them into some understanding in your lives and with direction for where you are going.

Not everyone will agree with them.

My understanding is to give you facts as I understand them myself. As to what is occurring around and on the earth during these next few years. These words are not to bring fear into people but an understanding of change, so they can grow with these changes.

Armageddon, as it has been preached, is not of my knowing. Change happens constantly and always has in the history of the Earth. The events that are coming with this wave of energy are bringing together everything that has happened since time began on your planet to the present day.

It is as though Karma on the planet needs to be rebalanced for these changes to happen. It is as though you are balancing all your Karma in one lifetime rather than taking many lifetimes to do it. It is the balancing of the law of cause and effect.

With that understanding there is not one person sitting here that hasn't experienced trials and tribulations, if I am put it that way. There is a need to get closure over things we have created over many lifetimes. This is because when the Earth changes occur, the frequency will not be able to sustain the old ways any longer. That is why Karma is being balanced in one lifetime rather than in many.

It is closure of the past ways, so it can move forward in the new way.

For those that can't; or are not prepared; or don't understand these changes; I hope that my teachings will bring some insight for a little information is better than none. I ask you to give it in guidance so it is not misinterpreted.

Those that can not deal with these changes have already written into their contract this lifetime to exit this life before these changes are completed. Those contracts were made before life began.

So with this understanding I want you to be aware that these changes will be for the better and the overall good for all sentient beings and the planet itself.

The higher frequency will bring you into alignment with your higher self to universal understanding, so that you can live you lives in harmony and peace and grow in spirituality and understanding.

Where this hasn't occurred there have been many wars, pollution, weather events things that have been discordant with the Universal Laws on your planet. As I say, I do not want to preach an Armageddon that is not of my knowing, rather than an understanding of change, change that will be of a cleansing if you want to call it that way. It will cause us to reach out more fully as human beings and as spirit to bring the two understandings closer together to bring purpose, direction and insight to the reasons why you are experiencing what you came here to do.

To bring that understanding forward for you as your lifetime finishes a fuller understanding in sprit of being involved in a lifetime in a limited frequency. That limited frequency has served much purpose for many millennia. You come to the third dimension or the energy of this earth plane many times. Some of you may be aware of that or some of you do not have that awareness.

I want to explain coming from spirit into this energy of the Earth field. Ultimately, so you can experience certain things in this frequency that you can not experience in a higher frequency. Although this may sound like a negative connotation it isn't. I hope you may understand that from here you can feel pain; here you can feel sorrow in a very profound way, in a physical and an emotional way.

You can't do that in the same way in a higher frequency because the higher frequency doesn't support that density. You choose to incarnate into a limited environment perhaps to understand pain. Most importantly to understand that pain and negativity is the vehicle that we choose to experience density so that we may grow in awareness and in light.

You know when you are sad or are in grief; you know when you have suffered loss and misfortune; when you have suffered which is the foundation of a human being that if you can move forward through it and out of it you can learn much about unconditional love.

For in those places of negativity you find out those who really love you are. You also understand compassion and the understanding within that of non judgment. If you have been judged you would not choose to judge others. If you have learned compassion through sorrow or loss, then you have more of the understanding of the nature of humanity, and sentient life.

You can take that knowledge with you into the higher frequencies because in that place when you are evolved enough you can create your self worlds and different scenarios that can play out within the Universe. So to understand light is to understand darkness. In the third dimension the physical body is the vehicle that you use.

The words that have been written, the script that has been typed and produced, in the form of that understanding, is that those changes are occurring partly to help shift the old ways, the old third dimensional energy, from our understanding.

The Earth has the need to heal. The Earth, however you address her, is sentient life, just as you are. It is life that sustains life. In the process of millennia that has built up and built up much harm has come to the Earth. The Earth is not trying to harm you or to harm life, it is trying to heal what has been done to it. I know I have spoken these words before to some of you and I will not spend a lot of time here but I just want to say that it has the right to heal.

All life has the right to do that to heal, move forward and evolve. That is what your planet is trying to do. In the areas where there have been over population; where there has been war; where there has been pollution; damage to the very Earth itself; or toxic plants have been grown; where pollutions have happened in the oceans; where there is oil and different fossil fuels that have been taken from the Earth; where minerals such as diamonds, gold, and different essences or ores are taken from the Earth; it has interfered with the balance of natural energy on Earth. Those things exist to support life.

Within that understanding the Earth is going through the processes of change and healing. For example, the hurricanes in New Orleans and the flooding there. When we look at the Gulf of Mexico, it is one of the most polluted areas on earth as far as oil rigs are concerned; as far as pipelines taking energy out of the sea and out of the Earth are concerned.

The Earth brought in the wind, brought in this weather pattern that was to bring a cleansing into this area. It had no intention of hurting life as we know it. It is not of that nature or of that understanding. Because it was a densely populated area, because of the pollution the effects of this hurricane and the flooding were quite profound. The Earth only wanted to try and cleanse itself from some of the stuff that happened in that area.

When you look at the Tsunami that happened, the pathway that it took went over areas that were densely populated areas. Indonesia is one of the most densely populated areas of the Earth. It went through Sri Lanka that has been at war for many years. It went into the South eastern coast of India where there has been unrest and politics play out, over population, pollution and different things happening. It then spread over some islands and then hit the east coast of Africa; we know there has been war there in recent years. The Earth was trying to cleanse itself.

The quake happened as the tectonic plates shifted in the ocean just off the coast of Indonesia. That was part of the natural process of the Earth re-aligning itself. It is as though its cells moved in these tectonic plates. The shift happened in part, because it needed to, it was a way of cleansing.

If you have an infection on your body that will grow and erupt, the infection will burst or expand in a way that it will need something to happen to cleanse it. It you were to look at a boil and that bursting, it is cleansing itself by that process though it may not be a nice thought to experience. The Earth is trying to do the same thing, if I can put it in that way for you to understand.

The text that we have written in this the fourth part of Universal Stretches is to try and bring an understanding to ordinary people. People like yourselves and as I have been in lifetimes too, that need to understand these changes are happening not **because** of them but around them because of the conditions that are in affect on your Earth.

It is to take the fear away and move forward with this change. Openly so you can become authentically true to the understanding of what you are as spiritual beings in a physical experience.

Lyn Inglis and Karen Barker

References

Andrews, T. (1995). Animal-Speak: The spiritual and
   magical powers of creatures great and small. St. Paul,
   MN: Llewellyn Publications.

Braden, G. (1996). Awakening to Zero Point: The collective
   initiation. Bellevue,WA: Radio Bookstore Press.

Hanh, T. N. (2005). Being Peace. Berkley, CA: Parallax
   Press.

Hanh, T. N. (1992). Peace is every step: The path of
   mindfulness in everyday life. New York: Bantam
   Books.

Lama, D. (2005). The Universe in a single atom: The
   convergence of science and spirituality. New York:
   Random House.

Virtue, D. (2001). The Care and Feeding of Indigo Children.
   Carlsbad, CA: Hay House Inc.

Virtue, D. (1997). Angel Therapy: Healing messages for
   every area of your life. Carlsbad, CA: Hay House
   Inc.